salmon in the trees

life in alaska's tongass rain forest

photography by amy gulick

illustrations by ray troll

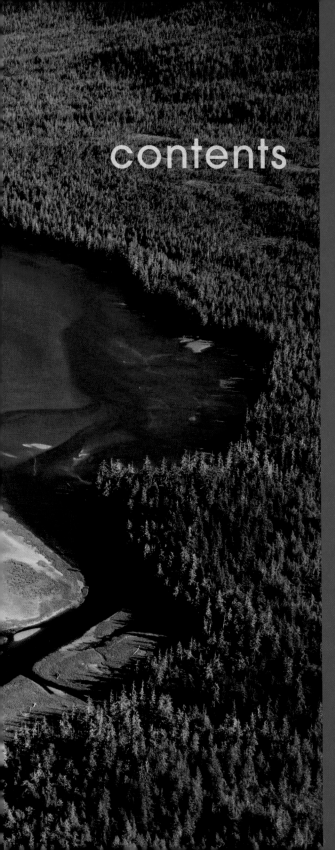

contents

www.salmoninthetrees.org

a letter from ketchikan

In the end, give
me rainy, strange,
bar-fight-nasty K-town
life with all its reckless,
unbounded chaos.

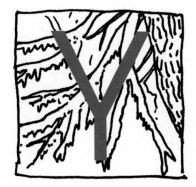

o John! Greetings from K-town by the sea.
You've often asked me why I choose to live
in the Tongass and I always say it was never
intentional, that I came here to spend the
summer working in my big sister's fish shack
on the dock in Ketchikan. One thing led to
another and twenty-five years later I'm still
here. So I guess it's obvious that what was once a capricious whim
became a firm decision.

Ketchikan is the perfect blend of wild and urban, which, in the end,
is its enchantment for Michelle and me. It's a town without pretense,
wearing its redneck heart on its sleeve—hard-working, blue-collar fishermen and loggers with a splash of yuppie cappuccino sippers like
me to keep things interesting. Add the lush lore of the Tlingit, Haida,
and Tsimshian and you have a vibrant, sensual brew. It's life in a place
assembled of mystery and mistakes that has made living here perfectly
reasonable.

Ultimately, what keeps us here is a raucous, unpredictable, sweet, and volatile collection of friends who move through the town's inconsistencies like fish in a stream. All of us seem to like that we can walk out our back doors and be lost in the deep forest in fifteen minutes. That inspires me and terrifies me, even when the politics get rancid. We only have about thirty miles of road to drive on and there are still only two stoplights in town. Escape ain't easy.

At times I've considered living elsewhere, including your town of Sitka. Once, we visited and stayed in a staid, fundamentalist bed-and-breakfast that felt like an *X-Files* episode and it totally weirded us out. I loved your beautiful volcano, the outside coast, and the centuries of history reverberating from every building, rock, and beach, but there was something a little too serious there for me, too much chin scratching and navel gazing.

It took me awhile to admit to myself that I need the strange funk of Ketchikan, that sweet uncertainty and mystery I mentioned to you earlier. In a moment that stunned me like an old friend I'd forgotten, who shows up unexpectedly, I realized I didn't think I could live without the stands of western redcedar that trickle out just north of Ketchikan. As they grow, they take on such ragged untreelike forms that they seem to be struggling with some unseen force that also makes its way into me. I knew I'd end up hankering for them. Our spruce trees are bigger than yours, too. You've got more snowcapped, jagged peaks and all that, and the giant brown bears. But in the end, give me rainy, strange, bar-fight-nasty K-town life with all its reckless, unbounded chaos. And besides, your high school's mascot is the wolf and ours is the mighty king salmon. In the end I'm a fish guy, so I've got to be true to my clan. I talked myself into a home, here, John, so I'll just sign off now.

As ever, your ratfish pal,

Ray Troll

PREVIOUS PAGE
Tongass Narrows

ABOVE *Walk Softly*

RIGHT Creek Street
in downtown
Ketchikan

what goes
around
comes aro

When we try to pick
out anything by itself,
we find it hitched
to everything else
in the universe.

~John Muir

AMY GULICK

rouched on a rock near a churning waterfall, I'm entranced by thousands of salmon thronging in a pool. Fin to fin, tail to tail, they sway against the current as one giant mob, like concert groupies in a mosh pit. I forget that they are individual fish until one springs from the crowded stream, hurling itself against the foaming wall of water. And then another, and another. Fish after fish, leap after leap, so much energy expended, so much energy delivered. The long green arms of Sitka spruce and hemlock trees spread across the stream as if to welcome the salmon back into their forested fold. Click, click, click goes my camera in a frenzied attempt to freeze an airborne fish in my frame. They're fast, much faster than my reflexes. I try again, and again. Hours vaporize, like the mist rising into the forest from the spray of the waterfall. But for the salmon every minute is precious because their time is coming to an end. They've

PREVIOUS PAGE Spawning salmon fight their way up Dog Salmon Creek on Prince of Wales Island. The word "salmon" comes from the Latin *salir*—to leap.

LEFT A bald eagle eyes a chum salmon in the Chilkat River.

RIGHT Some bears may eat their catch away from a salmon stream to avoid confrontations with other dominant bears.

stopped eating. They're in their final act—spawning—and they won't stop pushing upstream until they die. Their instinctive drive to pass on their genes is hammered home to me with every leaping fish. Click, click—lots of empty frames. I need to concentrate, but the distractions are many, and wonderful. The harpy screams of ravens emanating from the forest jolt my soul. Bald eagles swoop from treetops to rock tops, eyeballing the feast before them. Bears march into the stream with purpose, causing me to stand at attention. They know I'm here, but they seem focused on the fish at hand,

or at paw. With one eye pressed against the viewfinder, and one eye open for bears, I attempt to focus on anything but instead just bask in the present. I've never felt more alive. It's like I'm swirling in the middle of a wild performance with throbbing music, leaping dancers, and flashing lights. I have a front row seat to one of the greatest shows on Earth, one that plays out all over the Tongass every year.

Just a few days before, there wasn't a single salmon in this stream. In a few weeks, the only visible evidence of what took place here will be spawned-out carcasses

littering the streambanks. The cleanup crews of birds, otters, and mink will scour the remains. Heavy fall rains will wash the fish bones out to sea, and bears will curl up in their dens as snow dusts the mountaintops. The show will be over, but the annual payout is rich. Bald eagles, fueled by salmon, will soar greater distances to find food during the lean winter months. Female bears, padded with fat reserves, will give birth in their dens and nurse their tiny cubs with salmon-enriched milk. The forest, fertilized with supercharged soil from decayed fish, will sprout new growth come spring. And the salmon? Those who survived their time in the ocean, dodged the hooks, nets, beaks, and jaws of predators, and returned to their birth streams to spawn and die are still here. These salmon live on in frolicking spring cubs, plump blueberries, new growth rings in tree trunks, and downy eaglets perched in their nests. And the next generation of salmon is swaddled in the streams and incubated by the forest. The fertilized eggs will soon hatch, ensuring that the cycle of life is a circle, always flowing, never broken. In the Tongass, what goes around comes around.

The Tongass boasts nearly a third of all that remains of the planet's rare old-growth temperate rain forests, making it a world as well as a national treasure. Rarer still is that all of the pieces are here—ancient forests, wild salmon, grizzly bears, wolves, Steller sea lions, humpback whales, and more. The circle is whole. And we are part of it too, not strangers on the outside looking in. The Tongass is a place where people live with salmon in their streets and bears in their backyards. It's a land of remarkable contrasts. One of the world's largest densities of brown bears is twenty minutes by floatplane from the internet cafes and thirty thousand residents of Juneau, the state capital of Alaska. Cruise

Whitehorse

YUKON

BRITISH COLUMBIA

WRANGELL
ST. ELIAS
NATIONAL PARK

CANADA

UNITED STATES

Yakutat Bay

Yakutat

Alsek River

Skagway

Haines

Lynn Canal

Mendenhall Glacier

Taku Glacier

GLACIER BAY
NATIONAL
PARK

Glacier Bay

Gustavus

Juneau

ADMIRALTY ISLAND
NATIONAL MONUMENT –
KOOTZNOOWOO WILDERNESS

Icy Strait

State Capital

City

Wilderness Area

National Park

Indian Reservation

Non-National Forest Land within
National Forest Boundary

Outside National Forest Boundary

TONGASS NATIONAL FOREST

Hoonah

CHICHAGOF
ISLAND

ADMIRALTY ISLAND

Stephens Passage

TRACY ARM –
FORDS TERROR
WILDERNESS

Chatham Strait

BARANOF
ISLAND

Angoon

GULF OF ALASKA

Sitka

Frederick Sound

Kake

KUPREANOF
ISLAND

Petersburg

STIKINE –
LECONTE
WILDERNESS

KUIU ISLAND

MITKOF ISLAND

ALASKA

Summer Strait

Wrangell

ETOLIN ISLAND

Clarence Strait

REVILLAGIGEDO
ISLAND

MISTY
FIORDS
NATIONAL
MONUMENT
WILDERNESS

PRINCE OF WALES ISLAND

Thorne Bay

Klawock
Craig

Ketchikan

Hydaburg

Dixon Entrance

SOUTHEAST ALASKA

Prince Rupert

ships carrying more than two thousand passengers ply the same waters as mom-and-pop fishermen. That the modern world has arrived and hasn't yet broken the circle of life in the twenty-first-century Tongass is nothing short of astounding. But we're on our way to carving up this extraordinary forest, and it may just be a matter of time. We only have to look south to the once-magnificent salmon rain forests of Washington, Oregon, and northern California to see how quickly we can decimate ancient trees, wild salmon, and a rich way of life.

Not too long ago, we thought we could improve upon what nature had perfected. We put bounties on bald eagles and Dolly Varden trout, thinking we were helping salmon by killing their predators. We tidied and straightened salmon streams, not realizing that nature's chaos nurtures life. We built fish hatcheries and treated salmon like commodities instead of fine-tuned creatures that have carried their genetic message for millennia. We clear-cut ancient forests, not heeding the wisdom written in all those growth rings of trees many centuries older than us. We did all of this with the best of intentions, thinking we were doing the salmon, forests, and ourselves a favor. We know better today. That scientists have discovered salmon in the trees tells us that everything is connected. And if we start tossing away the pieces, we eventually unravel the whole glorious show. Salmon link the land to the sea and they can't survive if both aren't healthy. Neither can we. Long ago, we knew how to live within nature's constraints. Deep down, I think we still do. We need the Tongass, if for no other reason than to connect us to the world as we once knew ourselves. When the circle is whole, so are we.

We've been given a great gift, and an even greater responsibility. The Tongass is public land entrusted to all of us. All the pieces are still here. But for how long? The biological riches of the Tongass are vulnerable to the world's demand for minerals, timber, seafood, tourist destinations, and who knows what else down the road. Yet despite these threats, I have hope. I think we can get it right in the Tongass simply because there's still time to do so and we know it's the right thing to do. This is our time. Let us learn from the lessons that salmon in the trees teach us and ensure that the greatest show on Earth goes on.

seeing the
forest for
the fish

The bears,
eagles, and
trees here in
Southeast *are*
the salmon.

CARL SAFINA

That's gonna leave an ugly scar," says blonde-haired Brenda Schwartz-Yeager, a fourth-generation Alaskan commercial fisherman. "That logging was just last year." As we motor into the mile-wide channel separating Wrangell Island from the mainland, morning mists lifting from the island's slopes are revealing patchy clear-cuts. Fishermen aren't fond of clear-cutting. They know forests grow salmon. But the truth is more complicated, because salmon grow forests too. We'll take a closer look at that—because the salmon should be in the river.

Getting to Anan Creek from Wrangell takes an hour by boat. A few miles from town, big spruces and tall cedars rise thick on the steep slopes, each tree terminating in its own worshipful spire. Brenda is telling me she's tried living in several western states, "But after a while, you miss the wilderness, the fishing–. You think, 'Alaska isn't such a bad place to raise a

chittering of circling eagles fills the air, dominating even the proclamations of gulls and the croaking ravens. This place is as darkly near-to-enchanted as imagination can conjure. And that means it's a wild, dangerous place for those dwelling within—and perhaps more dangerous for those just visiting.

Brenda loads her rifle and we begin walking a path between the shore and the forest edge. Deep, opaque water flows swiftly through a 30-foot-wide channel between two bouldery banks. Every salmon entering Anan Creek must pass here. But this isn't their main gauntlet. After this narrow channel they enter a wide, shallow estuary whose bars are lined with eagles—dozens of them—and a few gulls. A brown bear (also called a grizzly) is walking through the braided shallows among the eagles. This ankle-deep stream is, in places, *carpeted* with salmon—pink salmon, about 5 pounds each—thousands upon thousands of fish. But even these shallows are not the main gauntlet.

We follow a trail imprinted with bear tracks. "Let's keep talking," Brenda says, "to let the bears know we're coming. You don't want to surprise one." She's telling stories of bears confronting people here, approaching with ears laid down, snapping their jaws, coming forward menacingly enough to generate warning shots near their feet. But no ugly contact, yet. Brenda's committed to keeping it that way. "If a bear appears on the trail, *do not run*. If you run, they're like puppies and will chase you. If you just stand there facing them, they'll have to think about what to do next. Then it will be very important that you follow my instructions."

More than usually aware of my surroundings, I notice that a lot of the place is *wet*. It really is a rain forest, and the line where sea meets land is blurry. Is the

PREVIOUS PAGE Bears play a significant role in spreading nutrient-packed salmon carcasses throughout the forest.

LEFT Annual rainfall levels in Southeast Alaska range from 38 inches in Angoon to 221 inches at Little Port Walter.

RIGHT Devils Thumb, a Coast Range peak on the border of Alaska and British Columbia, rises 9077 feet above Frederick Sound.

family.'" Now in her mid-40s, Brenda and her husband John are raising five kids aged 8 to 18. She's still a fisherman (the term most commercial fisherwomen prefer), and she's fishing more as her kids are getting bigger.

To the end of vision now, it's all water, trees, sky. The slopes ascend quickly into low clouds, and the clouds come cascading down in the form of near-vertical streams plunging into the trees.

~~~~~

We beach the boat near the mouth of Anan Creek and step into rain forest thick with undergrowth, full of ripe salmonberries, and cushioned with mosses. The

boundary the high-tide line, the mists, the trees, the paths of salmon, the flight ranges of fish-nourished eagles? The air itself is so moist, the frequent rain seems to just merge the land and ocean together. Some parts of Southeast Alaska get more than 200 inches of precipitation a year.

After the first wide channels, densely packed fish completely darken the stream bottom. It's as if black stones line the streambed—except the stones are actually fish. Only along the shore do the salmon part enough to let me see the light sandy bottom between them. Amazing.

Soon the stream begins ascending in a series of pools and low riffles. Another brown bear is at the lowest riffle, pulling on a salmon between the clutch of its claws and the clench of its teeth. Just ahead, the vegetation explodes as a black bear suddenly bursts across the trail, loping downhill toward the creek. I'm instantly flooded with adrenaline.

Anan is one of the few places where black bears and brown bears mix. Both can be dangerous, but the brown is less predictable, more confident, and justifiably more feared. Even black bears fear browns.

A few minutes farther upstream, two steep bouldery banks pinch the stream, and the constriction blasts a frothing torrent over a series of low falls. The falls impede the fish. Below this bottleneck, salmon are traffic-jammed shoulder to shoulder. *This* is their main gauntlet.

The falls are two-tiered. A fish must leap past the first fall and then immediately leap again, waging prolonged propulsion. Fish leap and fall back, leap and fall back, against the roar of opposing water. Many that make the first leap get washed right back to the starting

LEFT Humpback whale (*Megaptera novaeangliae*) diving in Frederick Sound

RIGHT Southeast Alaska is home to the largest breeding density of bald eagles (*Haliaeetus leucocephalus*) in the world.

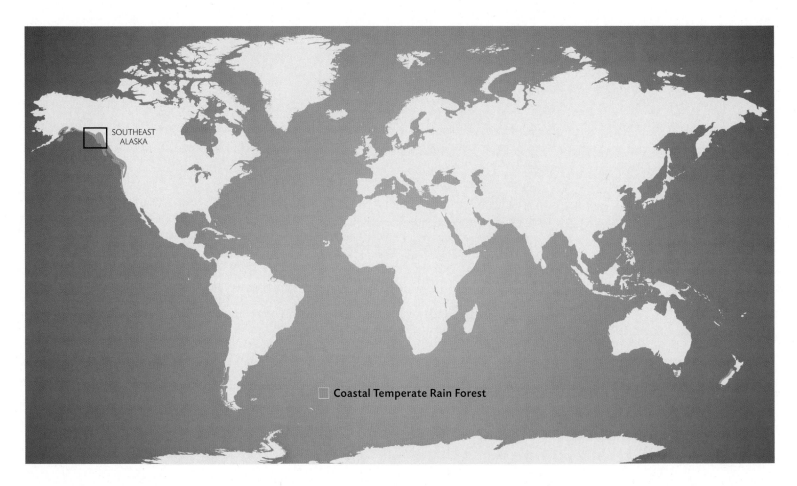

SOUTHEAST
ALASKA

☐ **Coastal Temperate Rain Forest**

gate. Any fish managing to surmount the falls must keep its motor revved through an intense run of white rapids stretching about 30 yards. Above that, finally, is a shallow, calm pool signifying success. But I see just one or two fish moving across that pool's light bottom. The great majority find the falls a serious inhibitor.

As youngsters, these salmon went to the ocean through this forest stream. Streams like this one, that draw from the mossy wet "sponge" of the rain forest, flow more evenly, more dependably. Shade helps stabilize and cool stream temperatures. Fallen logs form pools and eddies that break the current, giving rest and shelter to small fish, and—when channels flow hard with the swell of flooding rains—protecting the juveniles from getting prematurely swept seaward. Between the pools, currents in shallow riffles sweep away finer silts, exposing pebbles and cobbles where salmon can spawn—the spaces between stones hold their eggs, and the flow through the coarse streambed aerates developing embryos. Forests also produce flying insects, some of which feed young salmon. Salmon are here, in part, because of the trees.

MAP ABOVE **Global Distribution of Original Coastal Temperate Rain Forests.** Coastal temperate rain forests are rare, covering just one-thousandth of the Earth's land surface. (*Source: Map based on analysis performed by Ecotrust and published in 1995 in* The Rainforests of Home: An Atlas of People and Place)

RIGHT Where the forest
meets the sea

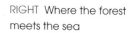

Big Bear Basics

DOUGLAS H. CHADWICK

Admiralty Island hosts one of the highest densities of brown bear populations in the world with one bear per square mile. Just across Frederick Sound, Kuiu Island supports the densest population of black bears ever surveyed. Other large islands in the Alexander Archipelago also have extraordinary concentrations of either brown bears or black bears. Surprisingly, no island hosts both, though browns and blacks share the mainland coast not many miles distant. It's a puzzle in biogeography that nobody has yet put

ABOVE Brown bear (*Ursus arctos*)

together. Does the curious mosaic simply tell us which species reached which island first? Or is there some special quality about certain islands that allows one animal to outcompete the other? Whatever angle you choose to look at the Tongass from, this is bear country like no other, and it adds up to one of the greatest crowds of big carnivores in the world.

Immensely strong, smart, inquisitive, and fierce, bears keep an unshakeable grip on our imagination, stimulating and inspiring us as few wild creatures on the continent can. But seeing bears as they really are, apart from all the myths and tall tales that surround them, can be a challenge. It doesn't help that the common names we've given these animals are somewhat confusing. Brown bears, *Ursus arctos,* found in western North America (and across Eurasia), can be nearly black, gold with chocolate legs, or platinum blond. Black bears, *Ursus americanus,* native to woodlands throughout the continent, also come in brown, cinnamon, tan, and palomino hues. One population along the British Columbia coast includes a large percentage of white individuals, popularly called spirit or Kermode bears. The Tongass mainland harbors another rare black bear

color phase known as the glacier bear or blue bear, whose grayish coat takes on an azure cast in certain lights.

Brown bears can be recognized by a muscular hump over the shoulders and a broader muzzle and face than typical black bears possess. While brown bears also tend to be bigger and more powerfully built, variations in age, diet, and genetics make size alone unreliable for identification. Monster brown bears exceeding 1500 pounds have been recorded, but so have adults weighing 300 pounds, half the weight of the largest black bears. The surest way to tell *americanus* from *arctos* is by the claws. Black bears have relatively short, curved ones designed to hook into bark, making it easy to climb trees. By contrast, brown bear claws grow so long—up to 4 inches—and comparatively straight that heavy-bodied adults lose the tree-climbing ability they enjoyed as cubs. These formidable nails are not used primarily for fighting or slashing prey, as folklore has it, but for digging up roots, tubers, and burrowing rodents.

On the basis of slight variations, taxonomists used to classify different groups of brown bears as separate species. These eventually got lumped into one, yet the experts continued to distinguish two subspecies in North America: those unique to Alaska's Kodiak Island, simply labeled Kodiaks, and the rest of North American brown bears. Generally, coastal bears are called brown bears while silver-tipped brown bears of the interior are commonly called grizzlies. These days, the two are considered merely different races, or ecotypes, of a single species, *Ursus arctos.* The Kodiak brown bear subspecies is *middendorffi* while the others are called *horribilis.* (That's right, *horribilis*; not exactly a case of science taking the emotion out of the way we define animals.)

As for why the Tongass is so full of bears to begin with, the explanation is a lot simpler. The place is permeated by streams, rivers, and inlets, and they teem with salmon. All five Pacific species, along with steelhead, arrive to spawn at intervals from spring through autumn. A good salmon run is beyond a banquet. It is a massive pulse of flesh, oils, and marine minerals that moves like rapids roiling upstream and literally spills over into the country-side, as exhausted and dying fish pile up along the banks. Feasting bears are giant boulders that part a river's currents. The bears trample the streamside paths into broad, muddy highways strewn with left-overs and dung, and they carry more carcasses deep into the forest.

Carnivores by anatomy, most *Ursus* are total omnivores in prac-tice. When not eating salmon sushi, they gorge on sugar-rich salmonberries, blueberries, elder-berries, and devil's club berries, all growing in rain-forest profusion. As you plow your way through thick vegetation toward the point of an estuary, everything you're stepping on is more summer bear fare: protein-laden sedges, wild members of the pea family, lil-ies with edible bulbs, and starchy roots and stalks of cow parsnip. The beaches below are loaded with seafood from tide-pool fish

ABOVE Black bear (*Ursus americanus*)

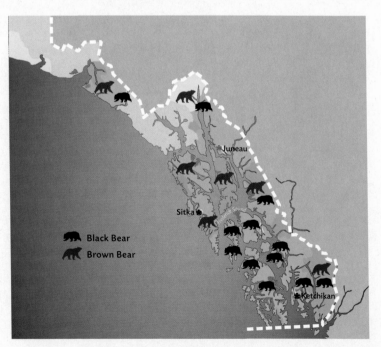

Black Bear
Brown Bear

Juneau

Sitka

Ketchikan

MAP AT LEFT Bear distribution in the Tongass

to clams. And all the way from tide line to high mountain meadows, the forests offer tender young grasses and herbs for grazing, not to mention a superabundance of deer to hunt or scavenge.

By the time Tongass bears are ready to den for the winter, their fattened body weight may be 50 per-cent greater than it was in the spring. That translates into high birth rates and high rates of survival from infancy to adulthood. The final result? The Tongass serves as a global stronghold for *Ursus*, black and brown. Black bears are fairly adaptable and can per-sist near settled areas. Brown bears don't do as well. They have already lost vast portions of their Eurasian homeland, 98 percent of their original numbers and range in the Lower 48, and are declining in major portions of Canada. In sections of Alaska such as the Kenai Peninsula, rising mortality levels as a result of increased bear-human interactions are a major concern. Brown bears need a true refuge from the modern world. If we had to pick one place where our children and the generations that follow them could count on being able to find an older world of huge trees, big leaping fish, great bears, and untamed spirits, it ought to be right here in the Tongass, where everything helps grow everything else.

Now, what if I told you that the trees are here, in part, because of the salmon? That the trees that shelter and feed the fish, that help build the fish, are themselves built *by* the fish? What if I said that?

It's not just rain that makes trees in the rain forest. Trees need nutrition. And the source of that nutrition is the biggest secret about the size, age, and extent of these forests. It's intuitive that the ocean creates clouds that deliver rain and that everything subsequently flows downhill to the benefit of salmon. Gravity, after all, isn't just a good idea—it's the law. Not long ago, everyone "knew" that nutrients—in the form of fallen leaves, for instance—flowed downhill, got into rivers, and were washed toward the sea. But ocean nutrients traveling *uphill*? And then out of the water, against gravity and into the forest? For a long while, no one thought to ask, "Hey, what about all these salmon?"

Salmon defy gravity by flowing uphill. And that upstream influx, that living flood tide, that *invasion* of salmon is energy—protein and fat and nitrogen and phosphorus. After spending years gathering the thin broth of ocean, salmon cease to be mere fish. They become delivery packages of super-concentrated nourishment. Other fish—like the candlefish (or eulachon)—also run upstream along the North Pacific coast. But for brute mass, nothing beats salmon. Salmon are the ocean incarnate feeding the forest.

Bears, eagles, and other middlemen sometimes take hefty cuts. In some streams, bears move more than half the salmon into the nearby forest. Follow this to its conclusion: Salmon make up a substantial part of the trees.

It's not that a forest *needs* salmon. There are plenty of forests where no salmon live or perish. But it's no

accident that some of the world's densest salmon runs and some of the world's lushest rain forests go together.

~~~~~~

Two black bears emerge from cavelike spaces between big boulders lining the opposite bank. Two others come from the woods behind us. Brenda and I watch from the tenuous safety of a low platform built specifically for viewing the drama. In addition to these four black bears, we're watching the large brown bear who's stripping another salmon just downstream.

That seems like a lot of bears—until the number of black bears increases to about seven adults, plus cubs. One mother has a set of cinnamon twins. Two other mothers have jet-black cubs. Another has a single youngster. Mothers with cubs seem uncomfortable about having their babes around other, potentially dangerous bears; they tend to take a fish

ABOVE Brown bear sow and cub catching salmon on Admiralty Island. Many species feed on salmon including bears, eagles, mink, river otters, gulls, sea lions, orcas, and humans.

and disappear into the privacy of the forest primeval, their little ones following.

Bears come and go from the shadows almost continually. I lose track of which I've seen before and which are new. Between their padded paws, the padded ground, and the sound of falling water, we never hear them coming. At one point I turn and am startled to see one walking right by me.

There must once have been a great many places like this, wherever creeks swelled with salmon, down the coast to California. Black bears live all the way across the

continent and must have once crowded even East Coast tributaries where American shad, alewives, striped bass, sturgeon, and Atlantic salmon came in vast schools to spawn. I try to imagine bears crowded along pinched arteries of the Hudson River in the spring of 1491. But what memory has recorded that? Where in the rocks is it written?

Meanwhile, so many fish fill this stream they hardly need to be "caught." When a bear steps into the water, salmon swim around its legs and under its belly. Bears just dunk

28

LEFT A commercial fishing boat "commutes" to work in Sitka Sound.

MAP AT RIGHT **Coastal Temperate Rain Forest of North America.** *Original Distribution: left map, Current Distribution: right map.* Close to half of the original coastal temperate rain forest of North America has been cleared for human development, agriculture, and commercial timber harvest. (*Map based on analysis performed by Ecotrust and published in 1995 in* The Rainforests of Home: An Atlas of People and Place)

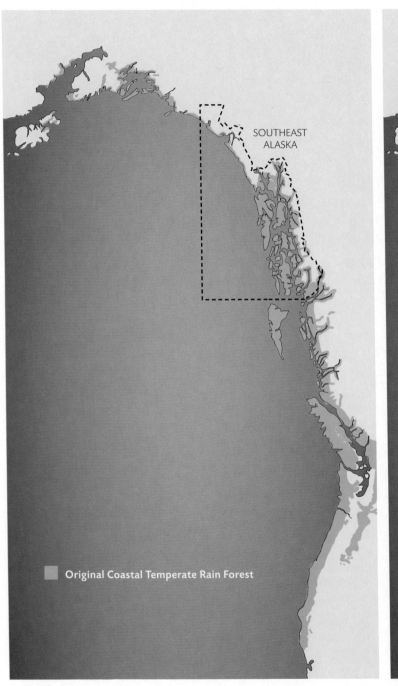

SOUTHEAST
ALASKA

■ Original Coastal Temperate Rain Forest

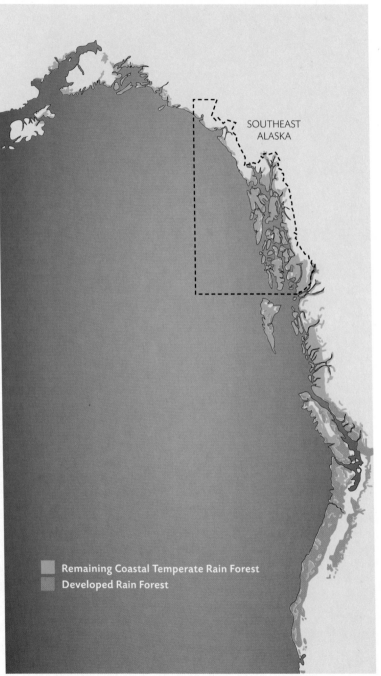

SOUTHEAST
ALASKA

■ Remaining Coastal Temperate Rain Forest
■ Developed Rain Forest

their heads and come up with their jaws around a wagging fish. In a fatal twist on catch and release, bears too full to eat pluck salmon from the throng, take a bite or two, and then release their grip. Sometimes a bear just drops a salmon on shore, abandoning it. Or a bear will carry a fish to shore and press on it to see if any eggs appear; if the salmon is a male or an unripe female, it usually gets left behind. By the end of the season following a good fish run, these fat bears, in some of the fattest bear country of all, can afford to be wasteful, self-indulgent, and picky—they abandon about three-quarters of what they catch and some seem almost bored.

Again a bear drops a fish on shore and then turns back to the stream and nabs another. Researchers say a bear might carry forty salmon from a stream in eight hours, leaving on the forest floor a couple hundred pounds of ocean essence in the form of rosy flesh. Insects, slugs, and other invertebrates move in and lay eggs. After them, the ocean-that-is-salmon then shape-shifts into insect-eating birds. More than fifty vertebrate land animals—even mice, even deer—nibble salmon.

Bears bring so many salmon into forests that the concentrations of nitrogen and phosphorus near some Alaskan streams exceed recommended concentrations for commercial fertilizer. Up to 70 percent of the nitrogen in the streamside foliage is of ocean origin—brought by salmon, delivered by bears, drawn into the roots of plants. Sitka spruces grow up to three times faster along salmon streams compared to streams without salmon. And this region harbors *eighty bears for every one* that lives in interior areas far from salmon streams.

So, why do bears feeding on abundant salmon often have three cubs? Why is the bald eagle more abundant here than anywhere else in its cross-continental range? Now you know: they are all salmon in disguise.

~~~~

Once upon a planet, the largest-treed, most fertile, most biologically massive forests in the world ran from Southeast Alaska all the way through northern California, in a land called the Pacific Northwest. This Alaskan end of that vast region still has the potential to maintain that heritage. In California, Oregon, and Washington, logging has cut down 95 percent of the original trees. Only a few trees survive that were already old when boatloads of Europeans reached what they pronounced a New World.

For those multimillennial trees, the last hundred years—when logging and dams blew the salmon runs to fragments—must feel like a morning with a missed meal. And there are consequences in this ad hoc experiment, a warning, a blinking red light that says, "Value what is here, or risk it all—and look to California, Oregon, Washington, and British Columbia for proof of ruin." Where there are no salmon, the forests don't get so lush and heavy.

Logging has hit the best forest stands of the Tongass hard too. But here there is still time to strike the right balance between people and the place. The places with the most salmon are most crowded with bears, most full of eagles, and grow the most massive woodlands. They all go together.

~~~~

That's nice, but a salmon's only concern is getting through to the spawning reaches. Because streams vary wildly in flow, length, grade, and the height of falls to be overcome, salmon vary widely in type and timing.

It's one thing to learn that some salmon are sockeye and others are pink, chum, chinook, or coho. To

RIGHT Like blood pulsing through veins, wild salmon infuse an upstream flow of nutrients into more than 4500 spawning streams in the Tongass National Forest.

Karl Jordan ~ Sitka

"It's one of the last places like it in the world."

The salmon engraved on Karl Jordan's wedding band reflects his family's way of life. A fourth-generation fisherman in Sitka, Jordan is proud to catch what he considers the best food in the world. "Many people want to be in tune with their food and know its story," he says. "When you have high-quality wild salmon, what else do you need?"

At 28, Jordan is more in tune with his connection to the natural world than people twice his age. His "commute" aboard *Sassy*, his 38-foot trolling boat, takes him past forested islands, rafting sea otters, and breaching humpback whales. He looks for seabirds feeding on herring, a good sign that salmon may be present. Weather, tides, and water temperatures guide his decisions. He knows he's part of an intricate web. "The salmon do us an awesome service by nourishing our bodies," he says. "And when they swim into the streams, they transport nutrients from the ocean and provide for the forest as well."

Since Jordan makes his living based on the number of pounds of fish he harvests, it's easy to think he would want to catch as many as possible, but he knows there has to be a balance. "A healthy natural environment provides a source to harvest wealth from," he says. "As fishermen, our economic viability depends on a healthy ecosystem."

He strives to maximize the value of each fish in order to operate as sustainably as possible. He'd like to take guests on his boat to experience a small-scale fishing operation. Many people would be surprised to learn that most of the wild salmon they order in a restaurant or buy at a market are caught by mom-and-pop operators like him.

Jordan has spent enough time outside Alaska to know how special his home is. Washington, Oregon, and northern California used to have bountiful salmon that supported a thriving fishing industry. Today, the salmon runs and fisheries there are just a fraction of what they once were. In these states, Jordan sees storm drains in the streets that are stenciled with "Salmon Stream. Don't Pollute." But in Southeast Alaska, he says, "you don't see signs like that. Instead, you see salmon everywhere, and you realize you're living in their territory."

He hopes people will see that the Tongass is a place where salmon can still thrive, and that the fish connect the land to the sea. "It's one of the last places like it in the world. It's not a tree farm and it's owned by everybody," he says. "I hope we can learn how to make a living by using the area as a savings account and making small withdrawals."

Since salmon have supported his family for four generations, he feels a responsibility to ensure that salmon can continue to thrive. He hopes his two young daughters will have the opportunity to become the fifth generation of fishing Jordans.

"It's a special lifestyle," he says.

ABOVE Commercial fishermen unloading
the day's catch of coho salmon

boost the confusion, most have two English names, thus: sockeye and red, humpback and pink, coho and silver, dog and chum, king and chinook. A stream might also have several seasonal runs of the same species—"the spring run," "the winter run"—each tuned and timed to specific requirements for streamflow, temperature, and nesting conditions.

Certain species range from the middle of the Pacific to the Continental Divide, accomplishing upstream spawning migrations of over a thousand miles *after* they hit freshwater—while fasting. Depending on who they are, the salmon may stay at sea for less than one year (pink) to seven years or so (chinook). They may attain adult sizes well over 100 pounds (which is why chinooks are called kings) or less than a twentieth of that. Chinook salmon spawn primarily in long mainland rivers with coarse gravel—the most challenging. Fishermen who sell direct to restaurants can get up to $30 per pound for a winter-caught chinook, making a single 20-pound fish worth $600. Pink salmon like these in Anan Creek spawn lowest and closest to the sea, so they are the youngest and smallest kind of salmon.

For all salmon, their lineage—the future of fish in Southeast Alaska—depends on getting to the right place at the right time. If they fail, their whole life will have been, from a salmon's perspective, for nothing.

The fish of Anan Creek still have to vanquish the falls. In late afternoon, the salmon seem newly motivated and the white water thickens with leaping fish. Many find themselves in a sheet of water falling over a slick-faced boulder. They skitter up into that falling water, swimming skyward against a pressure hose. They must act quickly before getting washed back down, and many fall back into the roiling eddies. The water seems

FISH·IN·THE·TREES

ferocious, almost hostile. How any of these fish can conquer this challenge is almost beyond reason. But nothing compels salmon to be reasonable.

I see a couple of fish get through. And then I see several gliding gracefully over the light sand of the broad shallows above, their goal—gaining the spawning reaches—now nearly assured.

~~~~~

Without bears, salmon would still die after spawning. Their carcasses would still draw eagles, gulls, crows, jays, and ravens. They'd still put smiles on the snouts of mink and marten. But without bears, most salmon carcasses that now find their way inland would wash downstream instead.

In the 1940s, fishery managers wanted bear populations thinned, or "culled," across Alaska. Why? Hysteria.

ABOVE *Fish in the Trees*

RIGHT By the end of the salmon season, bears favor the richest parts of the fish—skin, brain, and eggs—to put on as much fat as possible to survive winter hibernation.

LEFT Scientists have detected salmon, in the form of marine-derived nitrogen, in trees near spawning streams.

RIGHT Salmon carcasses, carried into the forest by bears and other animals, decompose and fertilize the soil. Trees and other vegetation then absorb the salmon nutrients through their roots.

Because salmon-eating bears were inflicting "economic damage." Because the great state might fall into "financial and social collapse" unless bears were killed. Fortunately, those bearish on bears got booed: the culling never happened. People had feared that bears limited the number of salmon. But the reverse is true: the number of salmon limits the number of bears. There are so many bears *because* there are so many salmon.

Bears make forests more productive by planting them with salmon. Productive forests put insects into streams, helping nourish young salmon and prompting rapid growth and a good start in life, helping keep salmon populations high. Abundance begets abundance. Thoreau's dictum applies: "In wildness is the preservation of the world."

The proof: These banks are lined with bears. This stream is packed with salmon.

〜〜〜

Just a few yards away, an adolescent black bear ascends a hemlock tree, seemingly just to take a rest. A little raccoon-size cub decides to follow it into the tree while its mother and sibling are at the creek. When the adolescent takes a swipe at the cub, the cub moves onto a lateral branch. From there, it can't get down. This is not trivial: cubs sometimes get killed when they find themselves alone with grouchy strangers.

Now we have a situation. The cub realizes it's stuck and begins bawling. Mother comes running back to protect her babe, bounding up the tree with astonishing speed. The adolescent, seriously threatened, begins snapping its jaws, stomping the thick branch on which it's standing, then urinating and defecating on the angry mama below. Complicating matters, her second cub has climbed a nearby tree, gotten stuck on a limb without

Brenda Schwartz-Yeager ~ Wrangell

"... there's something humbling about being in a real wilderness."

Brenda Schwartz-Yeager's ancestors worked as bounty hunters, trappers, and big-game guides on the Stikine River. Today, as a fourth-generation Alaskan, Schwartz-Yeager takes visitors to see the rugged beauty and plentiful wildlife of the area.

"I'm the first generation to be able to bring people here and not take anything other than photographs," she says.

Schwartz-Yeager's company, Alaska Charters and Adventures, specializes in small-group tours so visitors can have a genuine Alaska experience. Whether it's exploring the 335-mile Alaskan-Canadian Stikine River, dodging icebergs in the tidewater bay of the LeConte Glacier, or watching bears fish for salmon at Anan Creek, Schwartz-Yeager guarantees that no two days are ever the same.

"In society today, we're used to pushing a button and changing our scenery, the temperature, or the sound," she says. "We want to organize and control everything, but there's something humbling about being in a real wilderness."

As a child growing up in Wrangell, Schwartz-Yeager spent a lot of time in the nearby wilderness with her dad, a fisheries biologist and game warden. At times, her family shared their home with injured bald eagles and orphaned seal pups, and she assumed all kids had bears in their backyards. Her fondest memories are of times spent in some of the 150 public recreation cabins scattered throughout the Tongass National Forest. Today, at 44, she takes her own family to the cabins and guides visitors

to her favorite childhood places aboard her jet boat *Wild Side*.

Probably no other place she goes allows people to experience wild Alaska better than Anan Creek. Visitors walk through the rain forest and witness an age-old scene that plays out on rivers and streams all over the Tongass. Loads of salmon jam the creek, fighting their way upstream to spawn. The fish provide nutrients to the forest and also attract hungry critters of the feathered and furry kind. Bears are the star attractions.

"I tell visitors that we are guests in the bears' home, but I also want them to feel like it's theirs too," she says. "This is the Tongass—almost 17 million acres of their land, and I don't think they can care about it unless they feel some ownership."

Schwartz-Yeager thinks that places like Anan Creek and the Stikine River are valuable to her community because she and other charter companies can make a living guiding visitors to these unique and accessible areas.

"In Southeast Alaska, we're either going to cut a tree, catch a fish, or take you somewhere to see something. There aren't a lot of other economic opportunities," she says. "People here like where they live and will do what they can to stay. I think the Tongass can sustain different types of activities, and my hope is that people are able to use it in a variety of ways, including resource extraction. But all of this needs to take place in a manner that doesn't degrade the forest and the sea."

ABOVE Brown bear and kayak
on Admiralty Island

knowing how to get down, and is also bawling. This sends the now-distraught mother running from tree to tree, with Brenda and me almost directly in the middle.

Mama calls the second cub down, and they *both* climb the tree with the first cub and the adolescent stranger. Now all four bears are 20 to 30 feet up in the same tree. The mother wants the other bear away from her cubs. The other bear is threatened, scared, and highly conflicted. It wants to come down and flee, yet its escape is blocked by the mother. And the mother continues trying to press the stranger higher, away from her cubs. The more mama presses, the more defensive the adolescent gets. This standoff continues for about half an hour, until the mother presses the stranger still higher with a lot of snarling, jaw snapping, and lightning-fast bluffs designed to intimidate (which I find very effective). When she feels like she has enough space, she turns her attention to getting her cubs down. Then she too climbs down, and the threat is defused.

When everything is back to normal—normal for here, meaning the woods crawl with bears, the creek swarms with fish, and the sky is infested with eagles—Brenda and I, too, feel it's safe (enough) to head back down the trail.

~~~

The bears, eagles, and trees here in Southeast *are* the salmon. Flesh of their flesh. And before the salmon even hit freshwater on their way home to spawn, they have plenty of chances for reincarnation. Alaskan boats catch 80 percent of the salmon taken by fisheries on the entire west coast of North America. The fish also feed seabirds, seals, sea lions, porpoises, and killer whales.

It's all a great circulating pump of carbon, nitrogen, and other components, all the same and yet all representing a different moment of animation. Each element can seem different, or at odds, or in competition, but that's not all there is to it. The concern of individuals for themselves—whether a bear, an eagle, a salmon, or a person—hampers our ability to see the forest for the fish. Self-interest so blinds us to the big picture that we can't even sense that we can't really see, just as we perceive outer space as black when it's really filled with the light of uncountable suns.

Seen in new light, salmon become one long, self-propelled infusion. From the deep heart of the ocean, salmon beat their way upstream and inland like flowing blood, until—lodged in a thin film of water in a tiny tributary—each is a corpuscle in a capillary. These forests are where the ocean comes to die—and to be reborn. Take away the sea and there's not enough rain. Take away the fish and there's not enough food and fertilizer. The salmon are the ocean animated, part of the strangely wonderful, wonderfully strange shape-shifting sea-to-summit magic.

We can express gratitude to heaven for this gyre of life. Or we can demonstrate appreciation here, during our allotted life span. We don't need to "protect" what lives on here in Southeast. We just need to understand enough to avoid wrecking it.

～～～

Walking back to the boat with Brenda, I want to see another bear, but not just for the thrill. The animals don't seek thrills; wild things *pay attention*. Bears try to avoid trouble. So do I. But being in the wild sparks an alertness that feels alive inside me. Being here feels real because being here is real.

In every creation myth, people came into a world like this—rich, natural, but not without danger. The prospects for real trouble here are low, but the prospects for feeling alive are guaranteed if we make the investment.

I say, accept no substitutes for real living, real friends, and real bears. Either you set the bar high and keep it there, or you create a danger greater than any stalking bear: letting real life sneak away from you.

coming home: the land of old trees

Nowhere else in the United States do the most biologically productive landscapes remain in public ownership.

RICHARD CARSTENSEN

ne great way to appreciate your home is to leave it and then return. A few years ago I slowly drove a giant loop from my Juneau, Alaska, home to California and back. I brought 50 pounds of field guides and slept every night on the ground, immersing myself in the natural history of twenty separate ecoregions, geographies with distinctive climate and vegetation.

On the final leg of the sixty-day drive, I descended alongside British Columbia's Skeena River toward the coastal town of Prince Rupert, where the ferry leaves for Juneau and Southeast Alaska. Humidity grew palpably, and with imagination I could smell the sea. Ecologically speaking, I was home.

Southeast Alaska is the state's panhandle, climatically more like maritime Puget Sound than the frigid arctic conditions that most people associate with Alaska. Between the islands of the Alexander Archipelago

43

44

PREVIOUS PAGE Juvenile bald eagles perched on a snag on Mitkof Island

LEFT Johnson Cove in Moira Sound on Prince of Wales Island

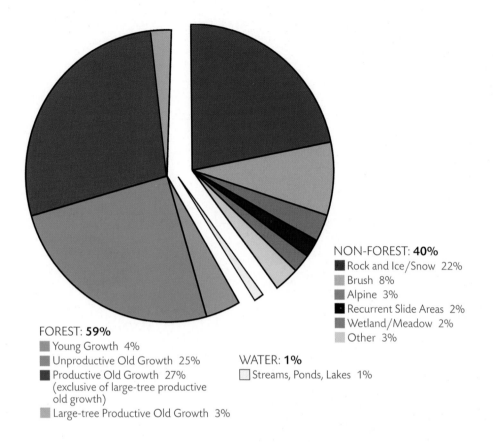

NON-FOREST: 40%
- ■ Rock and Ice/Snow 22%
- ■ Brush 8%
- ■ Alpine 3%
- ■ Recurrent Slide Areas 2%
- ■ Wetland/Meadow 2%
- ■ Other 3%

FOREST: 59%
- ■ Young Growth 4%
- ■ Unproductive Old Growth 25%
- ■ Productive Old Growth 27%
  (exclusive of large-tree productive old growth)
- ■ Large-tree Productive Old Growth 3%

WATER: 1%
- □ Streams, Ponds, Lakes 1%

ABOVE **Tongass National Forest Land Cover Types.** The Tongass National Forest is a giant mosaic of different land types, including forest, rock, ice, wetland, and water. (*Source: U.S. Forest Service*)

and the glacier-draped mainland ranges, there are 22 million acres in Southeast, of which the large majority are publicly owned: roughly 3 million acres in Glacier Bay National Park and Preserve and about 17 million in the Tongass National Forest.

Scanning the verdant hillside on the homestretch of my drive, I realized with a start that for the first time in 6500 miles I was looking at an unblemished expanse of old growth. A lover of big, old trees, I'd made side pilgrimages to ancient redwoods, sequoias, and Douglas-fir groves. But these were postage-stamp remnants, not visible from principal through-routes. In the Canadian

interior, I'd driven for hours through wild-looking country, scarcely passing another car, but fire keeps that dry northern forest young, setting back the successional clock every century or so.

Civilization and fire are the twin banes of old forest. Southeast Alaska and northern coastal British Columbia have almost no natural fires and a dispersed population of mostly small fishing villages. There are more acres of ancient forest than you could walk in a lifetime.

You can usually spot coniferous old growth even on distant hillsides or from a passing plane. Unlike younger forest, it has a ragged, unkempt appearance. Barkless, rotting snags stick up through the undulating canopy. Large gaps open where dominant trees fall, individually or in a domino effect. In contrast, young, even-aged conifers recolonizing after fire or logging are all about the same height. Not until a few centuries have passed is their smooth, tightly packed canopy broken by tree-fall gaps. Varied crown heights mark a forest of both young and old trees.

As I drove home beside the Skeena River, I felt both welcomed and sobered. The northern temperate rain forest could deservedly be named "the land of old trees." In my North Pacific Coastal Forests Ecoregion—alone on the continent—old growth is the thriving norm, not the vestigial exception.

That makes the Tongass an incomparable laboratory for ecologists exploring the role of deep age as a plentiful element in a healthy landscape. On my ecoregional comparison drive, I talked to one land manager in California's Central Valley who didn't even know what the original land surface of his refuge looked like, let alone the primal habitat mosaic. Was it wind-sculpted dunes? Scrawling San Joaquin overflow channels? All

A Forest of Islands

AMY GULICK

At twilight, a lone silvery wolf and I trade glances across the mirrored waters of Honker Lake on Prince of Wales Island. Five hours later, snug in my sleeping bag, I'm jolted awake by deep, drawn-out howls. I've heard this sound many times, but this is my first encounter with the Alexander Archipelago wolf (*Canis lupus ligoni*), a subspecies of the gray wolf. I'm lucky. While wolves are not uncommon in the Tongass, the chances of seeing or hearing them are slim. They are creatures of dim light and rugged terrain, and they inhabit certain islands but not others.

Islands define the Tongass. Sandwiched between the Gulf of Alaska and the jagged Coast Range on the mainland, more than five thousand islands comprise the Alexander Archipelago, the wolf's namesake and the heart of the Tongass. The islands that have wolves also have black bears, but no brown bears. The three largest islands that have brown bears—Admiralty, Baranof, and Chichagof—have no black bears or wolves. And the mainland is home to all three species. Islands are like that—places where a slew of factors determine who lives where. In the Tongass, deep straits with ripping tidal currents make it difficult for animals without strong swimming abilities or wings to disperse. This same obstacle is why the most reliable modes of transportation for people here are boats and floatplanes.

Just like the wildlife of the Tongass, island people are a unique mix. It takes a special breed to live a life that is both insular and vibrant, and many islanders told me they wouldn't reside anywhere else. There's something comforting about living on a hunk of rock where the rest of the world seems irrelevant. But islands have limits, both geographical and practical, and they make us think about how much we can take before diminishing a way of life for both wild and human communities.

Listening to the wolves, I think about my journey to get to Honker Lake: a two-hour jet flight from Seattle to Gravina Island, a five-minute ferry to Revilla Island, a three-hour ferry to Prince of Wales, a two-hour drive on former logging roads, now paved, to Hatchery Creek, and a six-hour upstream canoe paddle. Not an easy place to get to, and that's why the wolves are still here. Long may they howl.

LEFT Wolf fur and deer bones in the Honker Divide watershed on Prince of Wales Island

ABOVE Percy Islands. The more than
five thousand islands of the Alexander
Archipelago comprise much of the Tongass.

ANCIENT FORESTS FOREVER

ABOVE *Ancient Forests*

LEFT A large-tree old-growth riparian forest in the Honker Divide watershed on Prince of Wales Island

THE MAJESTY OF ROT

The Tongass is much more than forest. Of its 17 million acres, roughly half are forested, and about half of *those* contain trees of interest to loggers. Nonforested Tongass habitats include alpine tundra, ice fields, shrubby avalanche chutes, coastal meadows, and spongy peatland, too waterlogged to grow trees.

But the Tongass is best known—and rightly so—for its productive forest. The forest most valuable to loggers is, unfortunately, also most valuable to fish and wildlife. Figuring out how to live respectfully in this forest—building homes and heating with it, earning our livings in it, yet conserving what is now recognized as an international treasure—is the fundamental challenge of our ecoregion.

Rain-forest old growth is infinitely variable, but it's useful to think of two basic kinds: upland forest growing on hillsides of bedrock or glacial till; and bottomland forest growing on the deposits of streams and rivers, the well-drained and nutrient-rich material we call alluvium. The upland forest is dominated by shade-tolerant western hemlock and sometimes western redcedar. Alluvium more often supports large Sitka spruce.

Whether upland or alluvial, the forest at the heart of the Tongass timber controversy is massive, majestic, and rotten—not a good place for people hung up on tidiness or averse to parasitism. Moss-draped, fungus-riddled conifers stand so high their tops often can't be seen from the forest floor. The canopy is multilayered and structurally complex. The floor is strewn with logs in all stages of decay. If a hemlock or cedar is alive when it falls, hungry deer visit throughout the first winter, stripping off green needles. After several years, fine branches drop, then bark sloughs away. Within a few decades,

was remodeled by farmers' bulldozers before federal purchase of his bird sanctuary.

The World Wildlife Fund (WWF) estimates that the Central Valley Ecoregion has 0 percent intact habitat. No ecoregion I visited south of Canada had 25 percent. By WWF criteria, my ecoregion is 85 percent intact. This figure instills a sense of extraordinary privilege that deepens each time I visit the Lower 48 and return to the reassuring vista of ragged canopy.

mats of moss and tangled shrubs sprawl over the log as it relaxes into the waiting duff. Roots of young saplings hug and penetrate the rotting sapwood; the fallen tree is now a nurse log. A century later, it may be detectable only as a row of subtle lumps.

All features distinguishing old from young forest trace back in some way to tree decrepitude, mortality, or disintegration. What might be seen as loss for the tree is gain for forest habitat. Heart-rot cavities house woodpeckers, marten, owls, even bears. Brown creepers like to nest beneath a large flake of "delaminating" bark; vigorous young conifers don't provide this microhabitat. And only after centuries of staggered tree deaths does the forest achieve the kind of open, gappy canopy that allows shafting light to slip obliquely down to the understory, where key winter deer forage plants such as blueberry and five-leafed bramble proliferate.

What happens when we log such a forest or when a major windstorm knocks the whole thing down? While the initial scene resembles a bomb crater, in neither case does the forest start over completely from scratch. Soil, shrubs, and forage plants remain, and they flourish for several decades under warmer sunlight. Then—on most upland sites—young saplings that survived the chainsaw or gale close ranks as a tight, even-aged conifer forest with almost nothing edible on the ground. Upland and alluvial cut-over forests from zero to a hundred years old now occupy close to a million acres of federal, state, and private timber production land in Southeast Alaska.

THE HAMMERED GEMS
Between 1950 and 1980, industrial-scale logging targeted our most productive forest—the bottomland spruce type. On these streamside landforms, Sitka spruces commonly stand 50 percent taller than the hemlocks of surrounding uplands. I think of those valuable but vulnerable watersheds as "hammered gems."

For many years, I've explored the remains of this towering streamside forest. In 1996, with Sam Skaggs,

UPPER LEFT Fallen trees create gaps in the canopy allowing light to reach the forest floor and stimulate new growth, resulting in a multi-storied canopy of trees of all ages and sizes.

LOWER LEFT In a productive old-growth forest, the ground is strewn with logs in all stages of decay. A fallen tree becomes a "nurse log," providing nutrients for new trees growing on top of it.

RIGHT Many trees start their lives on top of a "nurse log," which eventually leaves a gap known as a "ghost log" once it has disintegrated.

Matt Kirchhoff, and John Caouette, I began a project called Landmark Trees—an attempt to document Southeast's finest surviving giant-tree forest. Over the following decade, we measured seventy-six 1-acre patches between Ketchikan and Juneau, the cream of their respective watersheds. We found spruces as tall as 250 feet and up to 11 feet in diameter. The alluvial forest is the heart of the Tongass. Most alluvial channels host salmon, the ocean's gift to land.

It's hard to imagine a resident species that doesn't benefit in some way from salmon, whether by direct consumption or elsewhere in the food web. Even animals that miss the annual pilgrimage to alluvial forest still cash in, thanks to the parade of salmon-derived nutrients that leave the streams on wings of birds, fins of flounders, and droppings of wandering bears. Underground, a network of braiding "paleochannels"—ancient streambeds covered over by more alluvium—stores and redistributes the wealth.

Beneath the tall, streamside spruces, heavily fruiting devil's club, salmonberry, and stink currant respond to sunny canopy gaps, reduced acidity, and groundwater-delivered nutrients. On larger or more dynamic streams, belts and islands of red alder colonize disturbed bars and terraces. A nitrogen fixer, alder may be as important as salmon to the enrichment of terrestrial and aquatic habitats. Before about 1950, alder was limited in distribution.

That changed with the onset of industrial forestry. Logging companies raced from one stream bottom to the next, stripping the great spruce forest from streambank to valley wall. What came back was mostly alder.

Walking those streams today can be depressing or exciting, depending on your values and open-mindedness.

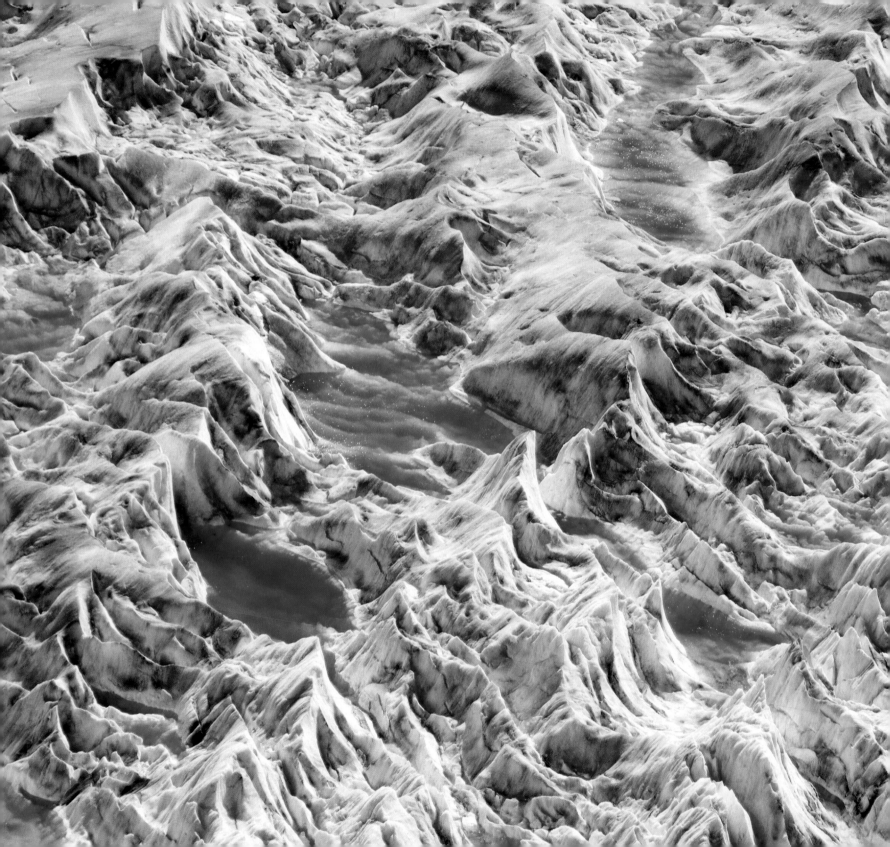

LEFT South Sawyer Glacier in Tracy Arm-Fords Terror Wilderness. About 40 percent of the Tongass National Forest is not forested and consists of ice fields, alpine tundra, avalanche chutes, wetlands, and water.

For a big-tree lover, the giant moss-covered spruce stumps are painful to behold. Having spent a decade trying to raise awareness of the magnificence of that mostly lost Landmark Forest, it took awhile for me to admit that the young trees now replacing it have already become rich habitat in their own right.

Alluvial second growth does not resemble the dark, dead-understory conifers that inherit upland slopes after logging. Many of our stripped valley bottoms have matured into a sea of deciduous alders. Spruces grow far apart, rooted on stumps and down wood, often suppressed for their first half century under the leafy canopy. Abundant summer greens and berry production continue to attract grazers and fruit seekers. Scattered throughout the sweep of young alder are patches of old growth that escaped the logging, critical wildlife refuges especially in winter.

The young alder forest is not ideal habitat for certain fish and wildlife species. Coho salmon suffer from loss of massive logs in the streams because their fry need deep pools and overhangs for winter cover. Even pink and chum salmon that don't overwinter as fry sometimes die before spawning if shade-depleted streams dry up. But in most years, pink and chum spawn in great swarms throughout the alder-lined cut-over valleys, in turn attracting everything from bears to mergansers to carrion beetles. The logged bottomlands continue to serve as nutrient-exporting habitats.

Another kind of hammered gem landscape is karst— the "swiss-cheese" topography that develops on soluble carbonate bedrock such as limestone and marble. On low-elevation karst such as northern Prince of Wales Island, trees once grew even larger than on alluvium. Spruces 10 to 15 feet in diameter, once fairly common, are now essentially gone. What's left in the remaining karst old growth are massive western redcedar and ancient yellow-cedars. Formerly considered trash wood, these cedar forests escaped the saw until recently. Unfortunately, they've now become our most valuable timber species. Most that I've encountered lately are in proposed cutting units, in watersheds that have already been heavily logged.

At the opposite extreme from the karst and alluvial hammered gems, in terms of forest productivity, is granite. Granitic bedrock breaks down grudgingly, forming sterile, acidic soils. The trees are generally scrubby, of little interest to loggers unless there's a lot of yellow-cedar. Our most spectacular wilderness areas are granitic: Tracy Arm, Misty Fiords, south Prince of Wales. This is also true of some of America's favorite national parks: think of Yosemite.

But you can't eat scenery. In Alaska as in California, we've developed our breadbaskets—the Central Valleys— and saved our splendid, sterile highlands. It's easier to save granite because it doesn't grow big trees.

GETTING IT RIGHT

So far, to the best of our knowledge, no species or subspecies has been driven to extinction by human activity in Southeast Alaska. Few ecoregions can claim this. But the future is precarious for some of our forest animals because of the way we logged. Even here in one of the world's most intact temperate rain forests, people have consistently high-graded, taking the best forest first. The relatively small percentage of Southeast that was logged included the majority of our most productive watersheds, those rich in karst or alluvium, with the ability to rapidly grow large trees.

ABOVE Ice cave in Mendenhall Glacier.
At the height of the Wisconsin glaciation
during the Pleistocene ice age, ice covered
nearly half of North America and most of
Southeast Alaska.

Becky Janes ~ Juneau

"We have pristine wilderness right out our back door . . ."

Twenty-thousand years ago, the land where Becky Janes' home sits was covered in ice more than 4000 feet thick. Today, she lives in a U-shaped valley carved by the receding ice, still visible as the Mendenhall Glacier.

"We have pristine wilderness right out our back door, and the glacier is recreation heaven," says Janes. "My husband and I hike the trails with our son and dog. In the winter, people cross-country ski on Mendenhall Lake and ice climb on Mendenhall Glacier and frozen waterfalls nearby."

Every year, tour buses bring more than 350,000 people to the Mendenhall Glacier in the Tongass National Forest. Just 12 miles from downtown Juneau, the visitor center overlooks a milky lake dotted with floating icebergs in front of the glacier. It's an incredible view, as close as most people will ever get—unless Janes is their tour guide.

Going above and beyond the usual glacier tour, Janes leads small groups onto the massive hunk of ice. Outfitted with crampons, helmets, and ice axes, visitors hike through

the forest that has sprouted since the ice retreated, then onto bare rock not yet covered with vegetation, and finally up to the frozen blue wall itself. With one small step, participants leave firm ground for a world of ice.

"To have an opportunity to walk on a glacier is a magical experience, and most people are blown away by it," she says. "I love taking people on the glacier and showing them what makes Alaska, and particularly Juneau, unique."

Janes, 29, and her husband were both born and raised in Juneau. They started their ecotourism company, Above and Beyond Alaska, in 2002 and cater to more adventurous people looking to get off the tour buses. With a staff of fifteen, the company guides visitors on low-impact single- and multiday trekking and kayaking trips. Of all the outings offered, the glacier hike gets the highest raves.

"The whole concept of the glacier trip—hiking out and back instead of flying by helicopter—is very rewarding and people love it," she says. "It's a perfect day trip for travelers to Alaska."

LEFT Brown bear watching for spawning salmon on Admiralty Island, home to one of the highest densities of brown bears in the world—nearly one bear per square mile.

RIGHT Neck Lake on Prince of Wales Island

At this northern end of the great temperate rain forest, watershed productivity is much less universal than in Washington or Oregon. Our large-tree forests were concentrated in a few special watersheds. To loggers they must have seemed like clustered berries, begging to be taken. The choicest fruits have fallen, but the picking goes on. Targets of high-grading simply shift: once the big spruces on karst and alluvium; now the ancient cedars on the central and southern islands.

Perhaps it was inevitable that the Landmark Trees project—a celebration of Alaska's greatest forest—would morph into something less congratulatory, more urgent. Several years ago, fellow naturalist Bob Christensen and I started the Ground-Truthing Project, the "eyes and ears in the woods for the Southeast conservation community." Our project has been sponsored and directed by the Sitka Conservation Society. We surveyed past and proposed timber sales from Prince of Wales to Chichagof Island.

We soon noted that the watersheds most immediately at risk are the hammered gems, where karst and alluvium once grew giant trees. Small pockets of old

growth do remain—densely laced with deer trails and bear beds—but their proximity to roads makes them commercially attractive. Cutting these last patches is like yanking back the life ring from a struggling swimmer. For me, the hardest part has been my growing consciousness of lost antiquity, of the carelessly concluded story in those tightly packed tree rings. As a logger friend says, "it takes a thousand years to grow a thousand-year-old tree."

Yet even in this sad news there's a silver lining, and it has to do with the resilience of the hammered gems, particularly the valleys with abundant alder. These places, for now, are reliable providers for subsistence hunters, sport and commercial fisheries, and, most importantly, a wide range of wildlife species that respond well to the seasonal flush of insects, fruits, and greenery in the young deciduous forest. I hold this discovery in joyful counterpart to the sadness of the vanished "ghost forest." It's as if I were watching a play in which the hero, thought dead, is found to still be breathing.

Two kinds of wildland gems remain at risk in the Tongass timberlands. First are the large, essentially intact landscapes: places like Cleveland Peninsula and Rocky Pass. These forests are generally of low to moderate productivity but are critical to wolves, goshawks, and other species that do poorly around people and need a lot of room to move. The second kind of gem is the hammered variety—highly productive places such as northeast Chichagof and southern Kosciusko Island.

Nowhere else in the United States do the most biologically productive landscapes remain in public ownership. First settlers always claim them, and today they host cornfields, tree farms, and suburban sprawl. Conservation biologists and land managers in the Lower

CLOCKWISE FROM TOP LEFT Lichens and mosses grow on live and rotting wood and can provide important habitat and food for wildlife. • Wild blueberries and salmonberries • Goldenrod spider (*Misumena vatia*) on yellow lady's slipper (*Cypripedium parviflorum*) • Bunchberry (*Cornus canadensis*) growing in forests provides an important winter food source for the Sitka black-tailed deer.

48 are working with the leftovers, prevented by astronomic land prices from incorporating rich, private-land gems into habitat reserve networks.

In the Tongass, the gems are still ours. Here, we have the very real hope and opportunity to weave an ecoregion's richest watersheds into a land-use strategy that honors productivity as well as intactness. It's our last, best chance to get it right for the rain forest and for future generations. If we succeed in the Tongass, I believe that someday landscape ecologists will flock here, as to a Rosetta stone, looking for guidance in the protection and rehabilitation of imperiled ecoregions throughout the world.

RIGHT Forest on north
Prince of Wales Island

Gordon Chew ~ Tenakee Springs

"...I hope that we all continue to think about the Tongass as a sustainable living thing..."

In 1999, Gordon Chew sailed to Alaska from Washington state on his 36-foot wooden sailboat. With his wife and two young children, he visited different communities in Southeast Alaska because the family wanted to settle in the area. On their way to Sitka, they docked in tiny Tenakee Springs to soak in the town's public bathhouse, fed by natural hot springs.

"We noticed signs on the community bulletin board for jobs," says Chew, now 52. "My wife immediately got a job as a teacher's aide. So we came here for a bath and never left."

With a population of a hundred or so, Tenakee Springs is a waterfront community on East Chichagof Island. The bathhouse serves as the social meeting place, and the town boasts a small mercantile, a bakery, and an artists' co-op. What the town doesn't have are cars. Residents walk and ride bicycles on an oversized trail that is the only "street."

"Everything about the people and lifestyle here appeals to us," Chew says. "Pods of orcas swim by our living room window. I'm a middle-class guy with waterfront property. There aren't many places in the country where I could say that."

A builder and shipwright by trade, he built the town's harbormaster facility and restored the 110-year-old St. Francis Chapel. He also builds houses and decks for residents. "There's a lot of reward living in a community where I can see the benefits of my work on a daily basis," he says.

Until recently, the lumber he used was shipped by barge from another town. Freight charges alone can total half the price of the materials, so it's difficult to keep construction affordable. He realized that if he could harvest and mill local wood himself, then he could save on shipping costs. He approached the U.S. Forest Service and together they agreed on a small local timber sale in a previously logged area with an existing road system. By selectively harvesting individual trees and not clearing the entire area, Chew is able to minimize his impact on the forest and preserve the stand for the future.

"I'm trying to create a more positive environment among timber users, timber providers, and the public. Even the staunchest supporters of the forest recognize that our culture uses timber, but we don't want to ruin our resources," he says. "My goals are to provide local timber for the local infrastructure, and to help support the town and preserve its lifestyle. And I hope that we all continue to think about the Tongass as a sustainable living thing, and not just a place for resource extraction."

ABOVE Tenakee Springs

UPPER LEFT Productive old-growth forests, with lush understory plants and downed wood, provide habitat and food for wildlife.

LOWER LEFT The Sitka black-tailed deer (*Odocoileus hemionus sitkensis*) is an important food source for wolves, bears, and local people. Productive old-growth forests are critical habitat for deer, particularly in the winter, when these forests provide abundant food and shelter from snow.

UPPER RIGHT A second-growth forest several decades after clear-cutting. Even-aged trees that grow after a clear-cut eventually create a closed canopy that shades out new understory growth and food for wildlife. It can take several centuries for a clear-cut area to develop the characteristics of a productive old-growth forest again.

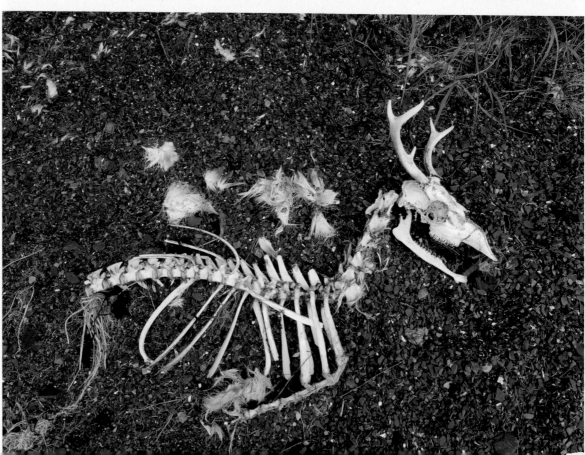

LOWER RIGHT Deer skeleton

LEFT Bald eagles fighting
over a salmon fishing spot

ABOVE Brown bear digging
for clams in a nutrient-rich
estuary on Admiralty Island

This is our home,
where the spirits of
our ancestors live and
where we trust our
children will continue
to live.

ROSITA WORL

ur oral traditions hold that we, the First Peoples of the Tongass, have lived here since time immemorial—or for more than ten thousand years according to the most recent scientific evidence. Our fervent desire is to live here for another ten thousand years and beyond. Our homeland in Southeast Alaska gives rise to our cultural values, which are grounded in a spiritual relationship to our environment, including all the living beings of the land, sea, and universe. The spirits of our ancestors also roam through our homeland.

We Tlingit are divided into two major groups, Eagles and Ravens, known as moieties. Each moiety is divided into clans, which are then further divided into house groups. Traditionally, Tlingit were required to marry someone of the opposite moiety, although this requirement has relaxed. However, children continue to follow their mothers' moiety, clan,

We are also children, not only of our fathers, but our father's entire clan. While we maintain autonomy within our clans, the intermarriage between Raven and Eagle clans unifies us as Tlingit People.

When I introduce myself I say:
Yeidiklas'akw ka Kaa.háni yóo xát duwasáak.
My name is *Yeidiklas'okw* and *Kaa.háni*.

Cháak' naa áyá xát.
I am an Eagle.

Shungukeidí naax xát sitee.
I am from the Thunderbird Clan.

Kaawdliyaayí Hit dáx áyá xát.
I am from the House Lowered from the Sun.

Jilkaat kwáan áyá xát.
I am from the Chilkat region.

Lukaax.ádi achxán áyá xát.
I am a grandchild of the Sockeye Salmon Clan.

My Tlingit name is *Yeidiklas'okw*. It is an ancient name, which is communally owned as real property by our clan. It has been handed down through untold generations until its meaning has been lost in the shadow of time.

My ceremonial name is *Kaa.háni*, which means "Woman Who Stands in the Place of a Man." This name recalls a historical event that occurred after the introduction of rifles into our society, sometime after 1741. It was obtained when we traveled inland to Canada to trade with our neighboring tribes. We exchanged rifles for furs that were piled to the height of a rifle, and a woman conducted the transaction, which was generally carried out by men.

and house membership, as did their mothers and their mothers before them.

Our clan memberships and names create bonds with our ancestors, who held the same names, and with future generations, who will also carry these names. This assures each Tlingit immortality through those who will carry their names. All members of a clan are viewed as kin even in the absence of a biological relationship. We see ourselves, not only as individuals, but as members of distinct social units through which we act collectively.

RIGHT Native girl at a pole-
raising celebration

Raven: The Trickster

RIGHT The Grand Entrance of Celebration in Juneau. Celebration is a biennial dance festival where Tlingit, Haida, and Tsimshian tribal members of Southeast Alaska gather to celebrate the survival of their cultures.

I am an Eagle of the Thunderbird Clan and the House Lowered from the Sun from Klukwan in the Chilkat region, which is in the northern reaches of the Lynn Canal in the north of Southeast Alaska. Although the larger society thinks of the Thunderbird as a mythological creature, we know that the Thunderbird is real and is near when we hear the sound of thunder, caused by the flapping of his wings as he flies, and when we see the lightning caused by the blinking of his eyes. He is the founder and ancestor of the Thunderbird Clan.

The name of our clan house, House Lowered from the Sun, derives from the story of a marriage between one of our ancient clan members and the Sun. She lived with the Sun but returned to our clan homeland when she became lonely for her family. To this day, our hair turns red as we age as a result of our ancestor living with the Sun.

Through my father, I am also a child of his clan, the *Lukaax̱.ádi*, or the Sockeye Salmon Clan of the Raven moiety. My grandfather's clan obtained the Sockeye Salmon as a crest when two of their young men fell off a canoe into the lake and were taken by the Sockeye Salmon to live with them.

Our clan crests are endowed with spirits, and in my case my spirits are the Eagle, Thunderbird, Sun, Killer Whale, Shark, White Bear, and those of my grandfather's clan, the Raven and Sockeye Salmon. Our crests symbolize our spiritual relationship to the land and our environment. Our claims to these crests and spirits provide an enduring link to our homeland and to our universe. We wrap ourselves in these spirits when we wear our ceremonial regalia, which are decorated with our clan crests and spirits.

Clan crests also reflect our history. For example, in the late 1800s a military officer known as Lieutenant Schwatga failed to adequately pay my great-great-grandfather, *Yendeiyánk*, for carrying the naval officer's supplies over Chilkoot Pass. Since names are considered real property among the Tlingit, *Yendeiyánk* took Schwatga's name and his uniform as payment for his debt, and today we Thunderbirds claim ownership of his name and wear the naval uniform as a crest. Other clans, such as the *Deisheetaan* and *Kaagwaantaan*, had encounters with the U.S. military and also claim ownership of the naval uniform for debts owed to them.

THE TLINGIT, HAIDA, AND TSIMSHIAN

Archaeological evidence found in a cave on Prince of Wales Island in 1996 indicates that indigenous people have lived in the Tongass for over 10,300 years. It is the aboriginal homeland of the Tlingit. The Haida Indians migrated to Alaska from the Queen Charlotte Islands off the British Columbia coast prior to the arrival of Europeans in 1741. In 1891, the U.S. Congress enacted legislation to establish a reservation for the Canadian Tsimshian people who migrated from British Columbia to Alaska.

Although we speak different languages, the Tlingit, Haida, and Tsimshian share a rich cultural tradition that evolved from the harvest of abundant resources of the Tongass and other areas of the Northwest Coast of North America. Such resources, most notably the harvest of salmon, allowed our ancestors to establish permanent settlements and to develop one of the most complex indigenous hunting and gathering societies in North America. The ancient forests of the Tongass also greatly contributed to our culture. The earliest European visitors were awed by the monumental totem poles in front of the large wooden, plank tribal houses, which could house up to one hundred tribal members. They were impressed by the 60-foot seaworthy canoes in which the Tlingit, Haida, and Tsimshian came to greet them with their songs and ceremonial oratory in languages they could not understand. These canoes also allowed our ancestors to traverse the coast from Prince William Sound to the northern coast of Oregon, a distance of some 1400 miles, trading for goods not readily available in our homeland.

CEREMONIAL LIFE

The persistence of our culture is most evident in our ceremonial life. When a clan member dies, we have a series of ceremonies beginning with the funeral or memorial service and a rite known as the Forty Day party. The

ABOVE Bald eagle on Sarkar Creek on Prince of Wales Island

LEFT *Daughter of Fog*

largest ceremony is the *ḵu.éex'*, which Westerners often refer to as a "potlatch." During this ceremony, we honor our ancestors and those in our clan who have died during the past year. Both Raven and Eagle clans sponsor these *ḵu.éex'* ceremonies, which are primarily held during the fall, and individuals from the opposite clans are invited as guests. We invite our ancestors and deceased relatives by calling out all their names and by displaying our regalia with our crests. Bowls of food, gathered from the bounty of the land and sea, are transferred to them in the spirit world by burning the food in a fire and by giving food to the guests. During this ceremony, we may also designate a new clan leader to restore the social order that was disrupted with the loss of our previous leader. Those of the opposite clans are repaid for assisting us after the death of our clan member. Members of

the host clans contribute sums ranging from $20,000 to $75,000. These funds, along with subsistence foods gathered from the land and sea, blankets, and a variety of commercial foods and goods, are distributed to the guests. Through these ceremonies, our bonds to other clan members are reinforced and our ties to members of the opposite moiety are renewed.

In 1982 our Elders—through our tribal organizations, the Sealaska Corporation (the Native entity created under the Alaska Native Claims Settlement Act of 1971), and the Sealaska Heritage Institute—implemented a new cultural activity, the first Celebration. Unlike traditional ceremonies, the Celebration is not clan-based nor are any ceremonial rites performed. Rather, we—as Tlingit, Haida, and Tsimshian—collectively participate in a dance festival to celebrate the survival of our culture through a tumultuous historical period, which began with the U.S. purchase of Alaska in 1867 and lasted through the first half of the twentieth century, when it seemed that our culture might be threatened with extinction. Missionaries, educators, and civil authorities alike saw our ways as heathen and deemed it best for us to learn the ways of the White Man. Many of our own grandparents, who saw the death of our culture as inevitable in the face of our land being expropriated and the wholesale repression of our cultural values and practices, also thought it best for us to adopt the Western culture.

Today the biennial Celebrations, which are held in Juneau, have grown to be the largest cultural activity in Alaska. In June 2008, twenty-three hundred dancers dressed in traditional regalia emblazoned with clan crests performed over a three-day period. More than six thousand Natives from throughout Southeast Alaska, including many of those who had moved away, returned home to celebrate and honor our traditional culture.

HAA AANÍ: OUR LAND

Southeast Alaska and the Tongass remain our homeland. Our traditional value of *Haa Aaní* expresses the duality of our relationship to the land in both "revering" and "utilizing" it. We believe that the land and all living creatures of the Earth and sea have spirits. When we use any natural resource, we must give thanks to the spirits and tell them how they will benefit our physical and cultural survival. When we cut a tree, we must lay a blanket on which it can fall and spread down feathers to ensure the safety of both the tree and those who are present.

A tangible sign of our spiritual relationship to the land, flora, and fauna is symbolized through our use of various plants. *S'axt'*, which is known as devil's club (*Oplopanax horridus*), has both spiritual and medicinal healing properties. We harvest it to make medicines and use the stalks in our houses and boats to ward off evil spirits. We even put devil's club in a canoe we made and sent to Washington DC in the summer of 2008. The canoe is on exhibition in the Oceans Hall of the Smithsonian National Museum of Natural History. We wanted to assure the safety of those who paddled the canoe on the Potomac River. Our Southeast Alaska Native Regional Health Corporation uses devil's club as its logo to signify its importance to our People. We have also resisted the commercial exploitation of devil's club until we are certain that the supply and our use are protected.

Our ancestors and shamans are buried throughout our homeland and within the Tongass National Forest. Our spiritual beliefs about the deceased differ

from those of most Western societies. We believe in the duality of spirits, with one dimension staying with the remains of our ancestors while the other travels to the land "Behind the Forest." When someone dies, we say, "He has walked into the Forest." Our Elders have directed that we do everything within our power to protect our burial sites, in particular those of our *Ixt'*, which is "One Who Walks with Spirits" but is most often translated in English as Shaman. The *Ixt'* has multiple spirit helpers, which remain at his or her burial site. Only his or her clan members are allowed to visit or care for the burial site. In 1998, the Sealaska Heritage Institute opposed the construction of a federal facility on the burial site of an *Ixt'* located outside of Juneau and has been seeking federal protection for the site, so far unsuccessfully. This concern for protecting sacred sites led the Sealaska Corporation to lobby for federal legislation that would allow Sealaska to acquire title to sacred Tlingit and Haida sites throughout Southeast Alaska under its Alaska Native Claims Settlement Act (ANCSA) land entitlement.

The land and sea are the basis of our traditional wealth and health and provide us resources for food, clothing, and supplies. Subsistence foods nourish our body and spirits. Our ancestors taught us that when the tide goes out, our table is set. We gather everything from red ribbon and black seaweed to clams, cockles, crabs, and a favorite we call gumboots or chiton. From the seas, we fish for salmon and halibut. We hunt for seal, which provides us with meat and fat, which we render into seal oil. We use the skins to make moccasins, vests, and other items. During the early spring, we lay hemlock branches along the beaches to catch the spawn of herring.

We gather a variety of berries and hunt for wildlife.

One of the most favorite is the deer, which is also important to our people as a symbol of peace. We share our subsistence foods with our family and friends and store the surplus for our fall ceremonies. Children are taught at a very early age about our cultural value of sharing, and they are required to share their first fish, or other resources they have caught or gathered, with their relatives. The harvesting of subsistence foods creates an obligation to share your bounty with your clan members and with Elders, and this act of sharing reinforces our social ties to one another.

Cherilyn and Marilyn Holter ~ Hydaburg

"Being Haida means knowing that when you share food it tastes better, not being afraid to grow old, looking forward to grandchildren with hope . . ."

When the tide goes out along the shores of Hydaburg village, the people go with it. They gather clams, gumboot chitons, and seaweed, just as their ancestors did since time immemorial.

"We have a saying that when the tide is out the table is set," says Cherilyn Holter, 42. "No one is hungry here. I live in the best place in the world."

Holter is a Haida Eagle of the *Kaachaadii* Clan. Raised in Hydaburg on Prince of Wales Island by her grandparents, she was surrounded by elders who taught her to gather traditional foods, weave baskets, and prepare and smoke fish. Occasionally, she heard them speaking in their native tongue. "When the elders didn't want me to know they were discussing me, they'd start talking in Haida," she says.

Although the language was not actively taught to Holter or her generation, she picked up a few words just by listening. On her first day of school, her grandparents told her not to use the words she'd learned because others would make fun of her. Speaking Native languages had been forbidden

or discouraged with the arrival of missionaries and government authorities in the 1800s, and Holter's grandparents were of the last generation to speak Haida fluently. By 1980, when Holter was a teenager, linguists predicted the Haida language would be lost in twenty years. Alarmed, she pressed her elders for more words.

"There are things that make us Haida—where we live, the food we eat, and allegiance to our people and culture. But how do you describe those things correctly without your own language?" she says. "When you hear stories and songs in Haida, it's much more dramatic or funny. You always lose something in translations."

While Holter can now read, write, comprehend, and with careful consideration speak Haida, she says she'll master it when she dreams in the language. For three years, she worked with linguist Jordan Lachler to help produce a two-volume Haida dictionary available on the internet. She teaches K–12 students the language and other cultural practices, such as weaving, singing, dancing, and gathering and preparing traditional food. Her hope is that the

Haida people will continue to enjoy the unique relationship they have with the land and sea, and that the things that have sustained her culture for thousands of years, like salmon and cedar trees, will still exist in four hundred years.

"No matter where you come from, you have to be proud of who you are," she says. "Up and down the coast, the Haida were the fiercest and most feared people. I feel like we're dormant right now and there's something huge we can give the world. Maybe it's just that we don't send our elderly away or we allow our children to get wet and dirty outside. Being Haida means knowing that when you share food it tastes better, not being afraid to grow old, looking forward to grandchildren with hope, and not ever taking anything for granted."

The Story of Haida Red

AS TOLD BY CHERILYN HOLTER

In Haida Gwaii (formerly Queen Charlotte Islands), about five hundred years ago, a sailing ship was found floating off the shores. It was an Oriental ship and there was only one survivor—a beautiful Oriental woman with red hair and light eyes. They said she was a supernatural being. She lived among the Haida and had three hundred Haida children by fifty Haida men. They called her Volcano Woman. Today, you always know the descendants of Volcano Woman by their red hair and light eyes, and you know they came from a supernatural being.

LEFT Totem pole in Sitka

The land also provides resources for us to make our art for which we have become internationally known. Women weave the wool from the Mountain Goat into the famous Chilkat robes. The trees from our forest are made into totem poles, canoes, masks, dancing staffs, ceremonial hats, and a variety of other art goods.

HAA SHAGÓON: OUR ANCESTORS AND OUR DESTINY

Our cultural value of *Haa Shagóon* ties the present generation to both our past and future. We have obligations to our ancestors and responsibility for future generations. The significance of this cultural value is practiced in multiple ways, such as basket weaving. When our ancestors gathered roots from spruce trees to weave into baskets, or hats and other objects, they did not take all of the roots but left enough to ensure that the tree would live and provide benefits for the future generation. We, who enjoy the benefits of their act, must likewise ensure that we protect our natural resources for future generations.

Our ancestors, over the course of thousands of years of occupation and migrations within the region, gave names to more than three thousand sites and features throughout Southeast Alaska. We developed a strong sense of ownership of the land. When Russia sold Alaska to the United States in 1867, our clan leaders met to decide how they would protect ownership of our land. Instead of waging a war they knew they could not win, they hired a lawyer and sent him to Washington DC to convey to the federal government that Alaska Natives owned the land; if the United States wanted to buy Alaska, they should buy it from the rightful owners.

The 1867 Treaty of Cession, the Organic Act of 1884, and the Statehood Act of 1959 acknowledged landownership rights of Alaska Natives but did not outline how aboriginal land rights would be addressed. In 1968, the U.S. Court of Claims paid the Tlingit and Haida Indians just over $7 million for the taking of lands within the Tongass National Forest and Glacier Bay National Park and Preserve.

In 1971, with ANCSA, Congress recognized our aboriginal title to the remaining land in Southeast Alaska but conveyed title to only a portion of our homeland. Our leaders wanted full ownership of our lands and promoted the use of corporations to implement the settlement. They rejected the reservation system under which the federal government holds lands in trust for other Indian tribes. Sealaska Corporation is now the regional entity in Southeast Alaska, and it owns over

ABOVE Spruce root and cedar bark are used to weave baskets, hats, mats, and other items.

ABOVE For the Native people, devil's club (*Oplopanax horridus*) is one of the most important of all medicinal plants, used to treat numerous ailments including arthritis, ulcers, and gastro-intestinal problems.

300,000 acres of lands and another 300,000 acres of village corporation subsurface lands. Village and urban corporations, which each received 23,000 acres, were established for thirteen communities in Southeast Alaska. Because non-Natives were the predominant population in five communities, Congress did not award land to the Natives within Haines, Tenakee, Wrangell,

Petersburg, and Ketchikan. Native residents there are still seeking their land entitlements in Congress.

CULTURAL SURVIVAL
Our identity was challenged by others who came to our land and who sought to eradicate our traditional culture. Our shamans were punished and sent to prisons

Carving Cultural Traditions

AMY GULICK

I step inside the carving shed and the pungent smell of cedar greets me. A tree that once stood in the surrounding forests rests on the floor, and Jon Rowan Jr., a Tlingit Eagle of the *Shank' Weidi* Wolf Clan, is carving it into a totem pole. It's one of twenty-one poles that he's overseeing the completion of for his village of Klawock on Prince of Wales Island. It's a ten-year undertaking, with 250 hours carved into each pole.

As I watch Jon and listen to his stories, it's hard to believe that the art of carving poles almost vanished. With the arrival of missionaries and government authorities in the 1800s, many Native practices were forbidden or discouraged; by the early 1900s, the totem poles, languages, and traditional ways of life were disappearing. Jon, 43, says that not too long ago the Native people in Southeast Alaska were hanging on to their cultures by their fingernails. But today, they have sparked a resurgence and totem poles now stand in parks, front yards, schools— even at the governor's mansion in Juneau. The town of Ketchikan alone boasts some seventy poles. Most are not museum pieces but instead are modern examples of a vibrant Native culture.

Jon hopes that Native youth continue their cultural traditions, and as the Native arts teacher for the K–12 Klawock school he's doing his best to ensure they do.

Carving alongside him is 15-year-old Noelle Demmert, a Tlingit Eagle of the *Kaagwaantaan* Clan. She's the lead carver working on a pole to honor a Haida man who carved a canoe for her village. Wearing a hooded sweatshirt and sporting bright red fingernail polish, she looks and acts like a typical teenager. Two months later, however, when I see her again at the pole-raising ceremony, she's a different person. Dressed in their ceremonial regalia, Noelle and Jon sing and dance among hundreds of Native people gathered for the celebration. Flowing button blanket robes, woven cedar bark and spruce root hats, and carved animal masks adorn and transform the performers. I feel like I'm watching something ancient, yet so alive and relevant today. But this is not a day of dancing for tourists.

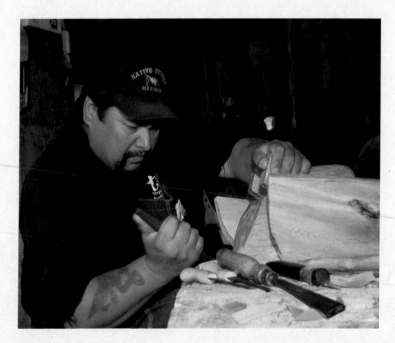

This is *their* celebration and I come to understand that the blood of their ancestors pulses strong in them, like the beat of their drums, like the salmon pumping up the streams that nourish their people.

As the pole is raised, the cedar tree stands upright again, strengthening a culture that has flourished along these forested shores since time immemorial.

LEFT Jon Rowan Jr., Tlingit Eagle of the *Shank'Weidi* Wolf Clan, carving a totem pole in Klawock

ABOVE LEFT Noelle Demmert, 15, Tlingit Eagle of the *Kaagwaantaan* Clan, carving a totem pole in Klawock

ABOVE RIGHT Noelle Demmert at pole-raising celebration

RIGHT Raising the pole

82

LEFT Totem pole in Kasaan
on Prince of Wales Island

ABOVE Native children at the Grand Entrance of Celebration in Juneau

RIGHT Singing at a pole-raising celebration

for practicing their trade. Missionaries and the federal government established boarding schools where Native languages and culture were not allowed. In 1944 I was kidnapped from my grandparents, who were living in Petersburg, and I was taken more than 100 miles away to a Presbyterian boarding school known as Haines House. My Tlingit mother (actually my biological aunt) used to "rent" me from this Christian school—or orphanage—so that I could spend time with her. It took my family three years to get me out of the school.

Fortunately, the Tlingit and Haida continued to practice their ceremonies, sometimes in hiding, as well as our subsistence economy and traditional harvests. We continued to make arts and crafts for the tourist trade. Though it seemed our culture might become extinct, the Tlingit, Haida, and Tsimshian recognized and valued their traditional ways of life.

The Southeast Alaska Natives organized the Alaska Native Brotherhood (ANB) in 1912 and later the Alaska

Native Sisterhood (ANS). Initially the ANB and ANS focused on securing landownership rights and civil rights. By the 1960s, a cultural renaissance was beginning, and Southeast Natives threw off the cloak of oppression and brought their cultural practices into the open. ANCSA provided the economic strength and organization for Southeast Natives to restore our indigenous language and to protect and revitalize our culture. We are also using our education to identify conflicts between our traditional values and the institutional forms we have adopted to serve us. We are examining ways to integrate our values into these modern institutions to ensure our cultural survival.

Our relationship to the land and to the Tongass is the basis of our cultural survival. Subsistence hunting and fishing nourishes our body and spirits, and sharing the bounty of the land with our family and community reinforces our clan ties. Our continued occupation of Southeast Alaska and our relationship and obligations to our clan and tribe explain why we have survived as Native People. Ten thousand Tlingit, Haida, and Tsimshian continue to live in Southeast Alaska and within the Tongass. This is our home, where the spirits of our ancestors live and where we trust our children will continue to live. We hold that the cultural diversity borne from the bounty of the Tongass is a resource to be protected for the country at large, for our People, and for future generations.

LEFT Totem pole on
Revillagigedo Island

RIGHT Dancing at a pole-
raising celebration

crossing

tongass narr

a journey

through time

OWS:

For as long as
there have been
people, they
have been coming
into the Tongass . . .

BRAD MATSEN

board the water taxi from the Ketchikan airport to town, I was falling in love with Southeast Alaska again after forty years of comings and goings. Flat calm water overlaid with the aroma of wood smoke, the cold-ocean tingle in the still air, and a fiery sunset up Tongass Narrows seized my senses with their messages of abundance and well-being. It was yet another in an endless succession of such welcoming moments that made Southeast the only real home I have ever had, the place over which my ashes will someday fly from the vent window of a floatplane. Lost in my reverie, I heard the ship before I saw it, a kind of basso rumbling just inside the range of audible sound that in a dark forest would have signaled primitive danger.

I turned to look and there it was, 900 feet long, bigger than the *Titanic*, its hundred-foot-high flanks aflame with sunset orange like it was creating the color instead of reflecting it. We were well clear so there was no danger,

but close enough so I could see the faces of hundreds of people standing at the rails, illuminated by the soft light of day's end. Couples on the ship huddled in embraces, others stood hand in hand, some were alone. Many waved. As Southeast Alaska slid out of their lives—for most of them forever—an overwhelming sense of joy showered down on me from the ship like a soothing mist.

A million cruise ship passengers come to Ketchikan every year on forty different ships making five hundred port calls. They absorb profound moments of joy, wonder, and amusement, and then leave. With the pulp mill closed and fishing nowhere near the source of cash it once was, Ketchikan has reshaped itself for dependence on the cruise ships, but not without paying a tremendous

PREVIOUS PAGE The view west of Craig on Prince of Wales Island

ABOVE Harbor seal on iceberg in LeConte Bay

ABOVE All of the straits and inlets of Southeast Alaska are glacial fjords. The South Sawyer Glacier in Tracy Arm-Fords Terror Wilderness is a tidewater glacier that ends in the sea.

price. For a century, the waterfront had been a symphony of diverse, home-grown businesses serving locals and seasonal migrations of loggers, fishermen, hunters, and adventurous tourists. Now it has been transformed into an industrial tourist processing plant that can handle five of the giant ships with their fifteen thousand passengers in a single day. Stores sell curios made in

China, gold jewelry from India, and totem poles carved in Bali with distinctively Indonesian features on the faces. At kiosks, bewildered tourists book tour packages by bus, boat, and floatplane into the Real Alaska and buy tickets to a logging show celebrating the old days. Most business owners relieve the cruise ship passengers of as many dollars as possible, board up their stores, and

LEFT Petroglyphs and pictographs are evidence of the ancient people who lived in what is now the Tongass National Forest. Petroglyphs (art pecked or ground into rock) are often found near salmon spawning streams facing the open sea, and may have welcomed the return of the salmon.

ABOVE Tlingits in ceremonial regalia for 1904 potlatch in Sitka *Credit: Alaska State Library, Elbridge W. Merrill Collection, Elbridge W. Merrill, ASL-P57-021*

wisdom of a practicing phenomenologist who just watches it all go by. "They're just another thing."

It has taken me awhile to realize that Bullet was right. For as long as there have been people, they have been coming into the Tongass, taking something, and leaving. The cruise ship passengers take beautiful, life-affirming moments like the one I had just shared with a bunch of them that sweet evening on the Narrows. Earlier swarms of people had come for food, gold, timber, and fish.

The next day, with Bullet's odd remark and one too many hours at the Potlatch Bar rattling around in my head, I was on the ferry with my pal Ray Troll, heading out to Prince of Wales Island to go fishing. Ray and I have been telling stories together for fifteen years, agreeing that being an artist and a writer are just socially acceptable ways to indulge our fascinations with fish, dinosaurs, geology, astronomy, or whatever else we happen to be interested in. Ray has lived in Ketchikan most of his adult life, rolling with the punches as a progressive liberal in a small town dominated by conservatives and people made desperate when the pulp mill shut down. Somehow, he has made it work.

Two hours out of Ketchikan, our ferry skirted Kasaan Island, a piece of the geologic puzzle wildly out of place that should have been thirty miles west of where it was. We had gone ashore there once to chip 390-million-year-old buglike creatures called trilobites out of the limestone remains of a Devonian reef, ending the day in the forest marveling at an ancient campsite. Thousands of years earlier, bands of *Homo sapiens sapiens*—our species—had huddled to get out of the weather. We saw the long logs they had tipped against the overhanging limestone for protection and the symmetrical soot

head south from October to May. The waterfront in winter is a ghost town. Worse, the ships foul the waters of the Inside Passage. Until 2001, when the state passed laws about the discharge of sewage and smoke into the waters of Alaska, the ships pumped, spewed, and otherwise soiled one of the last best places on Earth. It is an old pattern.

I looked away from the passing behemoth and tapped the water taxi pilot on the shoulder. "Bullet," I said—his real name is Rich Schuerger—"Those cruise ships are a real plague, aren't they."

"Not really," Bullet replied, with the offhanded

stains from their fires on the cliff face. Those people had come to gather food—stranded crabs and fish in the tide pools of the prehistoric reef, mussels and clams from the reef at low tide, and shoals of berries just inland—without which they would have perished. It was good living as things went back then. One of the truths about the time of superabundance is simply that there weren't enough human beings around to take more than the forest paradise could give. The feedback loops were very short and obvious: if you took too many fish from a particular creek, you starved or moved someplace else to give the watershed a rest. Now, if you take too many fish you just eat pork chops shipped in from two thousand miles away. Or, as we are finally figuring out, you try not to take too many fish. Or too much timber.

The limestone and the ocean were the keys to superabundance. The porous rock overlain with a thin layer of well-drained soil nourishes trees, ferns, sedges, and ground cover, and permits rain and snow runoff to easily etch channels that become caves, creeks, and rivers. Salmon reinhabited the watersheds when the ice retreated thirteen thousand years ago, and a host of other creatures also found perfect niches in the rocky bays and estuaries. Once part of the sea floor before the tectonic engine compressed and drove it to the surface, limestone defines the geology of a hundred or so islands and portions of the continental mountain range to the east. It asserts itself now in six gigantic formations wound like plaits of braided hair laid along the mainland. These six strands are remnants of distinct pieces of drifting crust that docked against the much older rock of the North American plate and fused together over the past couple of hundred million years. The rocks were once buried deeply and then were uplifted and exposed by erosion and glaciation. Their grain is consistently parallel to the long southeast-northwest axis of the Alexander Archipelago. One of the most obvious and beautiful fault lines in the world cleaves the entire assemblage in a fracture more than 250 miles

LEFT New fiddlehead fern unfurling in the spring

CLOCKWISE FROM TOP LEFT The rough-skinned newt (*Taricha granulosa*) secretes a poison through its skin that is toxic to most animals. • Otters, mink, and ravens carry mussel shells from the ocean into the forest. • The Prince of Wales spruce grouse (*Falcipennis canadensis isleibi*) is endemic to Prince of Wales Island and several nearby islands in the Alexander Archipelago. • Rosy twisted-stalk (*Streptopus roseus*)

long, now occupied by the waters of Chatham Strait and Lynn Canal.

The rocks of Southeast Alaska were also the reason for the end of superabundance when industrial humanity got around to the Tongass a little over a century ago. After Vitus Bering showed them the way, Russian fur merchants set up shop in Kodiak and on the outer coast of what would become Southeast Alaska.

They stayed for about a hundred years, but life in the new colony was too rough to attract a real migration. The few new people who came and went didn't disrupt the deep rhythms of the place. It took the flash of gold to make men crazy and bring hordes of them into the territory. Prospectors found dust and nuggets near Sitka in 1872, and then more at Windham Bay, but both of these were just preludes to what happened in 1880.

Katherine Prussian ~ Thorne Bay

"My hope . . . is that we are able to sustain the forest ecosystems and keep the local communities prospering."

Katherine Prussian knows a thing or two about water. She spent much of her childhood stomping through mud puddles in Ketchikan, one of the wettest communities in Southeast Alaska, with rainfall averaging 150 inches a year. Today, as a hydrologist with the U.S. Forest Service in the Tongass, she spends much of her time studying water—how and where it flows, and if it flows at all.

Prussian, 36, lives and works on Prince of Wales Island, the third-largest island in the country and a three-hour ferry ride from Ketchikan. North Prince of Wales is the most biologically productive region in the Tongass and nearly every waterway on the island does or once did support salmon and/or trout. But in the last half century, many fish streams have been damaged by logging and road-building activities. Close to a third of north Prince of Wales' productive old-growth forests have been cut, and more than 2500 miles of roads (most originally built for logging) crisscross the island. But where some see devastation from the past, Prussian sees hope for the future.

"Because there has been a lot of timber harvest and road building, there are a lot of opportunities for restoration," she says. "It's a prime time to establish a restoration economy—put people back to work with a different type of forest management."

A good example of this new economy at work is Fubar Creek in the Harris River watershed. The creek historically supported four species of salmon as well as

steelhead trout. But landslides in the valley and the cumulative impacts of three decades of timber harvest degraded the creek's fish habitat. Prussian spent almost three years doing site surveys, hydraulic modeling, flow and discharge measurements, and aerial photo interpretation to determine how to restore the creek.

"Restoration is kind of a new thing in this area," she says. "The Lower 48 has been doing restoration for quite a while, and we've been able to learn from past problems and do a higher level of design so we can have more successful projects."

The thorough design time paid off. Prussian hired a crew and they restored the creek to its historical path. Less than two weeks after the project's completion, six hundred adult salmon returned to the stream's main channel. Time will tell if steelhead trout, a species sensitive to disturbance, will make a comeback.

"It's a win-win situation. We're improving habitat and providing jobs," Prussian says. "My hope for the future of the Tongass is that we are able to sustain the forest ecosystems and keep the local communities prospering."

When she's not working with water, she's playing on it. She kayaks and explores beaches with her husband and two small children, and she enjoys the summer feasts of fresh-caught fish, crab, and shrimp.

"The bounty of the sea and forest—that's what I love about living here," she says.

ABOVE Kook Creek on Chichagof Island flows
through a system of caves and karst windows,
and supports both sockeye and coho salmon.

During the eight years after the Sitka discovery, fortune seekers dipped pans into every creek they could reach on foot from the ports where they landed. Then, on a stream at the base of glaciated mountains on the mainland, in the northern end of the panhandle, two of them found a bonanza. Near a Tlingit village called *Dzántik'i Héeni*—which means "River Where the Flounders Gather"—Joseph Juneau and Richard Harris found gold nuggets and collected a half ton of quartz ore. The quartz was salted with gold and it was seemingly endless, the largest low-grade ore deposit ever found. In a decade, dozens of mines and mills in the northern panhandle were pulverizing the quartz, sluicing the gravel, and producing millions of dollars of gold every year. At the discovery site, the first town founded after the purchase of Alaska from the Russians was named Harrisburg, and later Juneau. Before the end of the nineteenth century, the waters of the archipelago were alive with southbound gold shipments and northbound hordes of prospectors, miners, and merchants heading for the goldfields of the Klondike. It was the end of a place in which, for thousands of years, people had taken little more than what they needed to survive.

For a while, the gold blinded interlopers to all other possibilities for extracting wealth, but soon they came for the herring, salmon, and halibut. In 1890, Peter Buchsmann built a salmon cannery in the town that would later carry his name—Petersburg—and within a decade almost every navigable cove in Southeast Alaska sprouted a fish-processing plant. Packing ships sailed north in May, the captains became the superintendents of the canneries or herring-oil plants, and fishermen from as far away as the Sacramento River in

California—which had been quickly fished out—went to work taking every fish they could catch with absolutely no restraint.

Just after the turn of the twentieth century, when rumblings about turning most of Southeast Alaska into a national forest began, the fishing and mining were chugging economic engines with no brakes on their throttles to slow them down. Tlingit, Haida, and Tsimshian people, the original inhabitants of the forest and the limestone coasts, were fighting to hold their cultures and subsistence lifestyles together in the face of the onslaught from the south. All of the Natives, and the few independent hand-loggers already cutting trees, were afraid that the United States government was going to reach in and take over their lives and livelihoods.

To John Muir, Theodore Roosevelt, and other visionaries, the controlling hand of the federal government was exactly what was needed to slow down the runaway fishing and mining industries before they left Southeast Alaska in ruins. A lot of people also feared that when industrial timber cutting inevitably followed small-scale hand-logging, the forest itself would be decimated. Muir's travels in Alaska with the Harriman Expedition in 1899 convinced him that unchecked development of the region's vast natural resources would devastate the great forest, its people, and creatures. Muir campaigned tirelessly for conservation, stewardship, and reasonably paced development and gained the ear of an already somewhat enlightened Roosevelt.

At a meeting of the Society of American Foresters in 1903, Roosevelt described the primary goal of his forest policy: "You yourselves have got to keep this practical object before your minds: to remember that a forest which contributes nothing to the wealth, progress, or safety of the country is of no interest to the government and should be of little interest to the forester. Your attention must be directed to the preservation of the forests, not as an end in itself, but as a means of preserving and increasing the prosperity of the nation." Roosevelt, Muir, and other visionaries knew that the timber of what they called the Tongass Forest was a national treasure that could be cut down and grown again for centuries of profit, but they also knew that they had to protect it. Roosevelt created the Tongass National Forest by presidential proclamation on September 10, 1907. With the Alexander Archipelago

Jim Baichtal ~ Thorne Bay

". . . geology has a direct effect on everything it touches, from the plants to the water to the critters . . ."

As a young boy, Jim Baichtal collected rocks. But it wasn't enough to just find and identify them. "I started asking why the rocks were there," he says.

Today, as a geologist with the U.S. Forest Service, Baichtal is still asking why. He spends much of his time studying what lies beneath the surface of the Tongass, especially a distinctive topography called karst, in which the bedrock is primarily soluble limestone. As heavy rain seeps through the forest floor, it becomes acidic and dissolves parts of the limestone, creating complex underground drainage systems and caves. On the surface, karst lands are characterized by cave entrances, sinkholes, and rocky beachfronts with dished depressions and sculpted spires.

"The karst here is a beautiful blend of how geology has a direct effect on everything it touches, from the plants to the water to the critters that live in and on it," says Baichtal.

Some of the biggest trees in the Tongass grow on karst. The roots penetrate into the fissures of the limestone, which provide for excellent stability as well as drainage. The limestone also buffers the chemical makeup of the surface water so it's no longer acidic when it enters the karst stream systems. Once underground, the water stays a cool temperature, and aquatic organisms like insects and salmon thrive. Studies suggest that aquatic communities associated with karst are six to eight times greater in biological productivity than those in nonkarst areas, and this abundance works its

way through the food web to eagles, bears—and people. Evidence of early humans has been found where underground karst streams emerge along the coast.

Cave excavations in the karst lands of the Tongass have also changed what people think Southeast Alaska looked like during the last ice age, and Baichtal says he's honored to be a part of these findings. With the discovery of human remains 10,300 years old and animal bones older than 41,000 years, says Baichtal, "we now know that vast areas of the outer continental shelf were never covered by ice. The idea of a coastal migration route for the first North Americans arriving from Asia and traveling south down the continent has now gained acceptance."

"I like to interpret the land that people live on in a manner they can understand," Baichtal says. To that end, he helped design the Beaver Falls Karst Trail on Prince of Wales Island. The falls, discovered by Baichtal, drop 40 feet and disappear into a nearby cave. An interpretive boardwalk trail takes visitors through muskeg and forest and past sinkholes and collapsed channels on the way to the falls.

"I feel a strong responsibility to carry on the legacy of Teddy Roosevelt, Gifford Pinchot, and others who created the national forest system," he says. "The national forests belong to everybody, and people who will never come to the Tongass want to know it's being managed in a good way.

ABOVE El Capitan Cave on Prince of Wales Island is the largest known cave in Alaska and is one of the longest mapped caves in the Americas. Excavations of animal and human bones in El Capitan and other caves of the Tongass have led to important scientific discoveries.

Forest Reserve that had been created in 1902, the forest covered 6.7 million acres. In 1909, Roosevelt added another 8.7 million acres to the north.

The delicate balance of that enlightened vision held sway in the Tongass National Forest for forty years simply because the scale of the timber harvest prevented wholesale destruction of the old-growth rain forest, streams, and coastline. The forests of British Columbia, Washington, Oregon, and California were producing plenty of sawmill and pulp timber to satisfy demand, so the costs of operations and transportation in Alaska were more than the market would bear. In 1947, however, Congress authorized what it called a timber-first policy for the Tongass, granting logging a higher priority than fishing and mining, which were both laboring through drastic declines in profitability. To punctuate this new industrial policy, three years later the federal government awarded fifty-year contracts to harvest trees to Ketchikan Pulp Company and the foreign-owned Alaska Pulp Corporation in return for their agreement to build giant pulp mills in Ketchikan and Sitka.

Every year for the next forty years, 20,000 to 60,000 truckloads of giant conifers left Tongass slopes to feed the pulp mills. Many of the fine-grained spruce and hemlock elders that started life five hundred years or more before the United States even existed were pulverized and chemically transformed to make newspaper, rayon, cellophane wrappers, and disposable diapers. Ancient cedars, cut down in clear-cuts to get to the spruce and hemlock, were no good for pulp, so they were left where they lay.

It was just another thing, as Bullet said, but what began to change the equation was the human

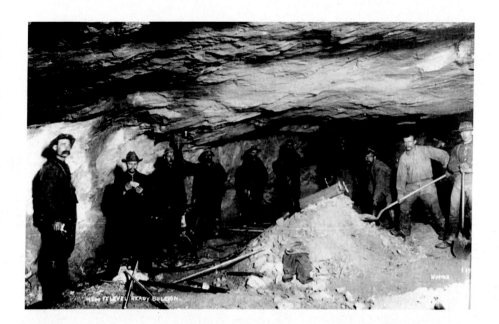

population that boomed after World War II. When I was born in 1944, there were 2.5 billion people on Earth. As I write this today, there are 7 billion and counting. It's a miracle, really, that there is anything at all left of the Tongass. In part as a matter of commercial self-interest to keep wealth flowing from the forest, in part as a response to the sheer beauty that we could not simply surrender into oblivion, we woke up to the fact that this marvelous place needed us as much as we needed what we could take from it. Slowly, the realization that a forest is not just trees crept into the awareness of the nation.

~~~

In 1971, the Alaska Native Claims Settlement Act (ANCSA) gave large tracts of the forest back to people whose ancestors had lived there for thousands of years. The Native corporations continued to cut the trees, in some places more drastically than ever, but at least it was becoming obvious to state and national leaders that handing everything over to two timber companies might need a little rethinking. The 1972 National Environmental Policy Act reached into the Tongass to demand that the consequences of timber cutting, road building, stream destruction, and the like had to be determined before extraction could begin. Four years later, the National Forest Management Act finally stipulated specific harvest and reforestation plans for the Tongass and every other national forest. In 1980, the Alaska National Interest Lands Conservation Act protected 5.4 million acres in the Tongass, including the Admiralty Island and Misty Fiords national monuments, from harmful development. Of that, 3.6 million acres—roughly 70 percent— are rock, ice, muskeg, and non-commercial forest. That act also set a 4.5 billion

board feet per decade timber supply mandate, along with a mandatory $40 million annual federal subsidy to do it, in part because of the increasingly restrictive regulatory environment.

In 1990, after a decade of activism to awaken the nation to the cascade of destruction wrought by industrial logging on the entire ecosystem of Southeast Alaska, Congress passed the Tongass Timber Reform Act. The act eliminated both the artificially high timber target of 4.5 billion board feet per decade and the $40 million annual subsidy that benefited the timber

ABOVE An Alaska State
ferry in Lynn Canal against
the Chilkat Mountains

RIGHT LeConte Bay in the
Stikine-LeConte Wilderness

companies, protected over 1 million acres of wild Tongass watersheds with vital community-use values, and required at least 100-foot no-cut buffer strips on all salmon streams. Three years later, in 1993, the Alaska Pulp Corporation threw in the towel, fired four hundred people, and shut down the Sitka pulp mill. The U.S. Forest Service responded by canceling the remaining years of its fifty-year contract with the company. In Ketchikan, Louisiana-Pacific, the owner of the pulp mill in that town, faced hundreds of millions of dollars in costs to bring it into compliance with more stringent environmental rules. The company fired five hundred people, shut down the mill, and left Tongass Narrows to the cruise ships.

After all of it, falling in love with Southeast Alaska over and over is as natural as breathing for me. On our fishing trip off Prince of Wales Island, Ray caught a monster 150-pound halibut and I managed to land a 24-pound king salmon. The fishing was spotty, but everybody knew it was way better than when the streams were damaged by uninformed logging practices and nobody was making the connection between salmon and trees.

There are more people than ever before passing through the Tongass—more than a million every year—and more claiming it as home. Some of them still cut trees, some catch fish, some just marvel at its beauty and the simple fact that it still exists. We are still taking, but we are more careful with our things.

LEFT More than 5000 miles of logging roads in Southeast Alaska have been constructed during five decades of industrial-scale timber harvesting.

UPPER RIGHT Industrial-scale clear-cut logging in the Tongass began in the middle of the 20th century after World War II. Clear-cut logging and its associated road-building activities reduce food and shelter for many wildlife species, and can cause soil erosion that may degrade salmon streams and sources of food, drinking water, and long-term employment for people.

LOWER RIGHT Forest service scalers scaling logs in rafts at the Ketchikan Pulp Company Mill in Ward Cove on Revillagigedo Island, 1957. *Credit: U.S. Forest Service, Prater*

ABOVE Glacier-sculpted
rock in LeConte Bay

RIGHT A pod of orcas
(*Orcinus orca*) cruising the
waters of Icy Strait

saving
the best:
a watershe
opportunit

> . . . Americans have the rare chance to help sustain the entire Tongass ecosystem—its fish and wildlife, wildlands, and wilderness values.
>
> **JOHN SCHOEN**

It was a calm morning with light drizzle from a low, ragged ceiling of clouds as I rolled out of my bunk on our boat anchored in Tenakee Inlet off Chichagof Island. Before I started the coffee, I got sidetracked counting bald eagles scattered across the tideflats at the head of Long Bay. I stopped counting at 168. I could also see six brown bears, including two sows with cubs, traveling upstream looking for fish. It was mid-August and the bay was full of pink and chum salmon migrating into streams to spawn and die, and ultimately to nourish a myriad of plants and animals in an intricate web of life that has endured for millennia. Such experiences are rare in the world today, but not in the Tongass National Forest.

The Tongass in Southeast Alaska is the nation's largest national forest and represents one of the last strongholds on Earth for old-growth temperate rain forest. With its thousands of islands in the Alexander Archipelago and about 16,000 miles of marine shoreline, dissected by glacial fjords and over 4500 salmon-spawning streams, the Tongass is renowned for its spectacular fish, wildlife, and wilderness. Unlike most forestlands in the United States—indeed, in most of the world—the vast pristine reaches of the Tongass encompass incomparable, intact watersheds, which still support all their native fish and wildlife species. Brown bears, wolves, bald eagles, marbled murrelets (a forest-nesting seabird), and all five species of Pacific salmon—rare or absent in their historical ranges farther south—still thrive in the Tongass.

Even so, the last half century of industrial old-growth timber harvest has brought significant ecological change to some of the region's most biologically productive lands. Logging in the Tongass has focused on the biggest, most accessible trees that grow in rich bottomlands—also the most valuable wildlife habitats. But industrial development in Southeast Alaska began a century later than in the Lower 48, and that gives Americans an unprecedented opportunity to conserve this remarkable rain-forest ecosystem and all its original parts.

Intact watersheds—from ridge top to ridge top and from the headwaters of a river to its estuary—are the key to maintaining the health of the Tongass. When conservation is addressed at this large, landscape scale, the entire watershed benefits—multiple species, complex food webs, and the full range of ecological processes are all preserved. Disturbances from road building are minimized, leaving diverse habitats whole and unfragmented—essential for wide-ranging species like brown bears and wolves, placed at risk elsewhere by increased human access. Salmon can carry essential nutrients upstream unimpeded, transferring them to the forest

when they spawn and die. All parts of the watershed are represented in their natural abundance, enhancing overall ecosystem resilience. Just as important, a fully functioning watershed is a scientific benchmark for monitoring, understanding, and managing environmental variability, such as what might happen with climate change.

For more than thirty years, I have been active in wildlife research and conservation in the Tongass, and during the last three I have conducted aerial and on-the-ground surveys as part of a five-year conservation assessment of the region. The aim of this effort, coordinated by Audubon Alaska and The Nature Conservancy, is to identify and conserve the most biologically productive

PREVIOUS PAGE Port Houghton is important habitat for brown and black bears, marbled murrelets, steelhead trout, and sockeye, coho, pink, and chum salmon.

ABOVE *The Salmon Life Cycle,* Smithsonian National Museum of Natural History

RIGHT More than 9 ft. in diameter and nearly 200 ft. tall, one of the largest Sitka spruce trees (*Picea sitchensis*) in the Tongass stands near Tenakee Inlet on Chichagof Island.

watersheds throughout the Tongass. The project ranks the value of individual watersheds to various species, looking at how much habitat exists for deer, bears, marbled murrelets, and salmon, as well as at the distribution of estuaries and large-tree old growth. Watersheds are ranked within each of twenty-two provinces distributed across the entire region—such as east and west Chichagof Island, Admiralty Island, and north and south Misty Fiords. The central belief is that ecological integrity —sustaining all ecological parts and processes—can be most effectively maintained by protecting healthy and whole watersheds throughout each geographic area of the forest.

Tenakee Inlet, Saook Bay, Port Houghton, Cleveland Peninsula, Rocky Pass, and Honker Divide are some of the most biologically productive and intact areas that remain in the Tongass. In protecting them, Americans have the rare chance to help sustain the entire Tongass ecosystem—its fish and wildlife, wildlands, and wilderness values.

TENAKEE INLET

The west side of Tenakee Inlet, including the adjacent watersheds of Goose Flats and Long, Seal, Saltery, and Crab bays, is a conservation priority area for the East Chichagof Province (which includes eighty-three watersheds) as well as for the entire northern Tongass. These contiguous watersheds provide valuable habitat for brown bears, black-tailed deer, marbled murrelets, and spawning salmon. People living across the inlet in Tenakee Springs also use the area for hunting, fishing, and recreation. The priority watersheds here support estuary habitat and stands of rare large-tree forests. In fact, during a survey of Crab Bay, a stand of big trees was

Salmon Time

AMY GULICK

Cruising up Chatham Strait, I jerk my head in all directions as hundreds of salmon erupt from the sea like popcorn bursting into the air. It's salmon time in the Tongass. A time when bears get fat and fishermen don't sleep. A time when eagles shriek and creeks sing. A time to indulge my taste buds.

In Sitka, I ask a local where to go for the best salmon in town. He advises me to meet someone fast and get invited over for dinner. Luckily, this isn't difficult. People are generous with the bounty in this fruitful part of the world. In Craig, a charter boat captain treats me to grilled coho brushed with a pineapple glaze. At a Native gathering in Kake, my entire being purrs upon savoring king salmon still warm from the smoke-house. In Hydaburg, a family serves me smoked sockeye, pickled wild beach asparagus, and Yukon gold potatoes. Kings and queens never had it this good.

I start an informal poll and ask everyone I meet if eating salmon ever gets old. Everything in moderation, right? Wrong. Not a single person hesitates before answering with a definitive "no." For me, wild salmon is always a treat. For the people in Southeast Alaska, it's a way of life. Summers are spent catching, cleaning, smoking, freezing, and canning for personal use. The commercial salmon industry is a mainstay of the local economy and has been certified as sustainable by the Marine Stewardship Council. Catch numbers, area openings and closures, and fish politics are headline news.

I like this way of life—spending time harvesting, preparing, and sharing delicious and nutritious wild food. It feels right. It builds community. It builds entire cultures—just ask the Native folks. To the wild salmon of the Tongass, I bow my head in respect and thanks.

GRILLED WILD ALASKA SALMON

Wild Alaska salmon is so flavorful that to serve it with competing flavors is to disrespect the fish. The key to good salmon is to buy it as fresh as possible, be sure that it's wild caught, and know that it tastes best when shared.

    Wild Alaska king or sockeye salmon fillet, skin on
    Light-tasting olive oil
    Brown sugar
    Paprika
    Kosher salt
    Black pepper

Rinse the salmon and pat it dry. Brush both sides of the fish lightly with olive oil. Sprinkle brown sugar and paprika evenly on the flesh side, gently pressing the rub into the fish. Top off with a little salt and pepper. Sear the salmon on a hot grill, flesh side down. Carefully flip the fish over so the skin side is down. Remove the salmon from the grill when white opaque droplets begin to form on the fish. The flesh should be firm on the outside but still a little rare in the middle, as it will continue to cook after it's off the grill. Take great care not to overcook the fish. Enjoy!

RIGHT Canning smoked king salmon at Dog Point Fish Camp

found above the beach, including a huge Sitka spruce 9.5 feet in diameter and over 190 feet tall—one of the ten largest known trees in Alaska.

Prior to industrial-scale logging, numerous trees in Southeast Alaska measured over 12 feet in diameter. Today, even trees 8 feet in diameter are exceedingly rare. Protecting this biologically rich area of Chichagof Island will ensure that fish and wildlife populations continue to flourish and will provide diverse economic, subsistence, and recreation opportunities for local people, as well as a unique place for other Americans to visit and see their public forest in full splendor.

SAOOK BAY

Twenty miles south of Tenakee Inlet, on northeastern Baranof Island, is another conservation priority watershed. Baranof is the most topographically rugged of the island provinces, and its scenery and wilderness are arguably some of the most spectacular in the Tongass. Alaska Audubon and The Nature Conservancy have ranked Saook Bay as the number-one watershed in terms of habitat values in the East Baranof Province. The watershed encompasses a substantial tidal estuary, a salmon-spawning stream, upland forest, and rugged alpine habitat to elevations above 3500 feet.

ABOVE The rich estuary of Saook Bay on Baranof Island supports Sitka black-tailed deer, brown bears, marbled murrelets, and coho, pink, and chum salmon.

MAP AT RIGHT **Examples of Conservation Opportunities within Biogeographic Provinces.** The opportunity exists to maintain the ecological integrity of the Tongass rain forest for the benefit of both human and wild communities. (*Source: The Nature Conservancy and Audubon Aaska, 2007*)

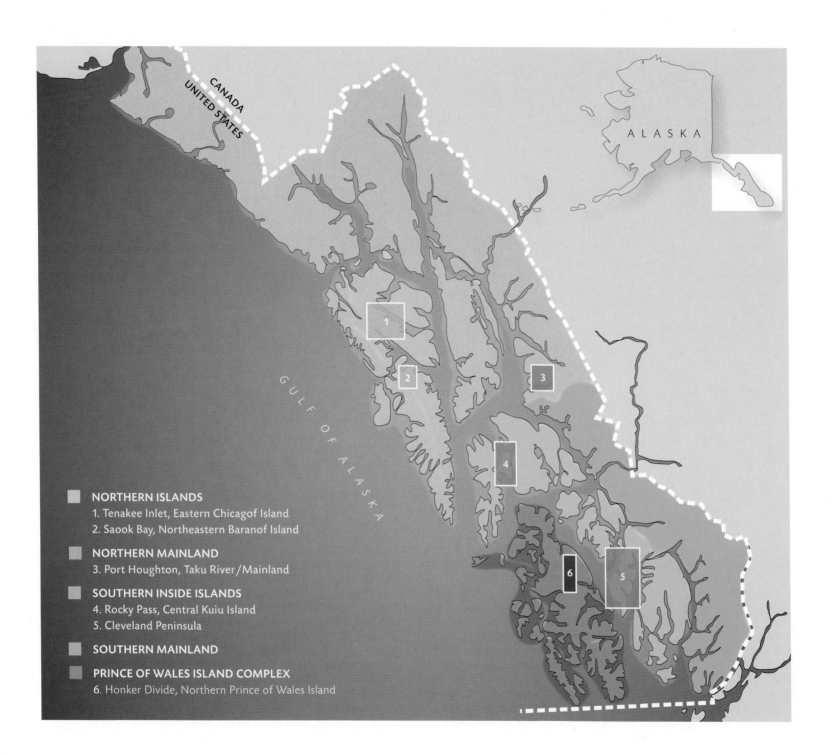

CANADA
UNITED STATES

ALASKA

GULF OF ALASKA

■ **NORTHERN ISLANDS**
  1. Tenakee Inlet, Eastern Chicagof Island
  2. Saook Bay, Northeastern Baranof Island

■ **NORTHERN MAINLAND**
  3. Port Houghton, Taku River/Mainland

■ **SOUTHERN INSIDE ISLANDS**
  4. Rocky Pass, Central Kuiu Island
  5. Cleveland Peninsula

■ **SOUTHERN MAINLAND**

■ **PRINCE OF WALES ISLAND COMPLEX**
  6. Honker Divide, Northern Prince of Wales Island

Michelle Masden ~ Ketchikan

"The Tongass is vast, beautiful, and diverse, and I love how free it feels to fly through it."

A self-described "flight junkie," 47-year-old Michelle Masden has spent seventeen thousand hours, or almost two years, above the Earth's surface. Her addiction to flying started early in life. As a young girl, she frequently traveled alone on commercial flights from her home in Nebraska to visit family in Illinois. Because she was a child traveling solo, she was looked after by the flight crew. "At the end of each flight, they always tried to give me a stewardess wings pin," she says, "and I would always tell them I wanted the pilot's wings."

At age 16, she took her first flying lesson. Her grandmother Esther, who was terrified to fly and never once boarded a plane, paid for the lesson. By the time she was 17, Masden earned her pilot's license. Six years later, she came to Alaska for a summer and never left.

Lured to Alaska by its wild grandeur, she started out working as a deckhand on a commercial fishing boat. But her desire to be in the air was strong. She watched seaplanes, the predominant aircraft in Southeast Alaska, take off and land on the water. "Coming from the Midwest, I had never seen a seaplane, but after taking a flightseeing tour in one I decided this is what I would do," she says.

Today, Masden's charter business, Island Wings, has been up and flying since 1993. Her passenger list

is as varied as the terrain she flies over in her seaplane *Lady Esther*. She transports campers and hunters to remote areas, facilitates aerial surveys of wildlife with biologists and Native people, and shows tourists the beauty of Southeast Alaska.

The most popular trip Masden makes is a two-hour flight-seeing tour to Misty Fiords National Monument, near her home in Ketchikan. Misty Fiords covers almost 2.3 million acres, most of which is designated as a wilderness area, within the Tongass National Forest. Glacier-carved granite valleys plunge to deep salt-water canals, and the area is home to an incredible array of wildlife, including bears, wolves, and mountain goats. It's not unusual for Masden to make the trip five times a day, and yet she never tires of showing others the spectacular beauty of the area.

She recalls one time when she landed in a cove with a group of tourists. They were all standing on the floats of the seaplane when a humpback whale surfaced so close that it blew mist onto the wings of the aircraft. On another occasion, a mother grizzly bear with two cubs fed just 60 feet from her plane.

"The Tongass is vast, beautiful, and diverse, and I love how free it feels to fly through it," she says. What does Masden do on her rare days off? Flies, of course.

"Passion is good fuel to get you through life," she says.

ABOVE Port Houghton on the
northern mainland coast

LEFT Big John Bay estuary in Rocky Pass between Kupreanof and Kuiu islands. The rich estuaries and small islets of Rocky Pass support an abundance of wildlife.

Although the lower drainage sustained some historical logging, this scenic watershed maintains high habitat values, ranking in the top five out of twenty-two watersheds in this province for deer, marbled murrelets, bears, and salmon. The Saook stream system provides spawning habitat for coho, pink, and chum salmon, which in turn become food for brown bears and other wildlife. This drainage also supports important stands of floodplain spruce forest with large trees.

At the head of the steep-walled bay, a luxuriant salt-marsh estuary leads to an islandlike knoll with centuries-old, large-diameter Sitka spruces overtopping a jungle of devil's club, salmonberry, and currant shrubs. Threading through this lush habitat are well-used bear trails—hiking them when bears are fishing for salmon is a hair-raising, adrenaline-filled experience.

PORT HOUGHTON

East of Saook Bay, on the northern mainland coast dominated by steep rocky fjords and interspersed with tidewater glaciers, is a pristine watershed in a remarkable setting. Port Houghton lies south of Juneau and extends 15 miles from its mouth along Stephens Passage to the entrance of a salt chuck, or tidal basin, nestled into steep forested slopes adjacent to ice fields and precipitous 8000-foot mountains along the Canadian border.

In mid-August, I was anchored in the North Arm, just outside the salt chuck and next to a large salt marsh. The tide was flooding as I headed up the narrow tidal channel in a small skiff. I watched a Steller sea lion catch a salmon and, once inside the salt chuck (2 miles long by 0.75 mile wide), passed a small island with seventy harbor seals hauled out and fifteen bald eagles in the trees. At the head of the salt chuck, a black bear fished

for salmon in the river. At least seventy-five eagles and one hundred harbor seals, plus several sea lions, were in the salt chuck. Outside the salt chuck, marbled murrelets occurred in substantial abundance throughout the inlet.

Moose, wolves, and brown bears also occur in Port Houghton, and the watershed supports good runs of sockeye, coho, pink, and chum salmon, plus steelhead. It ranks in the top 5 percent (out of fifty-seven watersheds) of the large mainland Taku River Province for marbled murrelet and bear habitat as well as for large-tree forest and estuaries.

ROCKY PASS

Rocky Pass is a narrow channel separating Kupreanof and Kuiu islands in central Southeast Alaska. Years ago, I cruised south through Rocky Pass—nearly 20 miles long and less than 100 yards wide in places. This was an extraordinary experience. The waters wind through a maze of rocks, islets, tidal flats, and rich estuaries that provide key habitat for an abundance of marine fish and invertebrates, shorebirds, sea ducks and waterfowl, eagles, and a variety of coastal mammals, including harbor seals, river otters, marten, mink, black bears, and wolves. At anchor one evening in Stedman Cove, at the north end of the pass, I heard calls of varied thrush and common loons and watched large flocks of mew and Bonaparte gulls. The hills were shrouded in fog, with patches of sun coming through breaks in the overcast. The evening light illuminated yellow rockweed along the beach and highlighted spruces and hemlocks frosted with chocolate-colored cones, all reflecting in the mirrorlike gray water.

Nowhere is the critical overlap of marine, aquatic, and terrestrial ecosystems so pronounced as in Rocky

LEFT Scarlet paintbrush (*Castilleja miniata*) in Yes Bay on Cleveland Peninsula. The peninsula is home to Sitka black-tailed deer, brown and black bears, all five species of Pacific salmon, steelhead trout, wolves, and mountain goats.

ABOVE The marbled murrelet (*Brachyramphus marmoratus*) is a seabird that often nests in structurally complex old-growth forests miles inland from the coast. The female lays its single egg on a mossy branch high in the forest canopy, and both parents fly from the forest to the sea and back to capture baitfish to feed the chick.

Pass. The east side of Kuiu Island and west side of Kupreanof Island host upland habitat that includes at least twelve salmon-spawning streams. This biologically rich area ranks in the top 10 percent (out of thirty-five watersheds) of the Kupreanof-Mitkof Province for overall ecological values and ranks first for black bear, black-tailed deer, and estuary habitat.

Rocky Pass encompasses the ninth-largest estuary in all of Southeast Alaska, which is the largest island estuary in terms of salt-marsh vegetation (about 800 acres). Coho, sockeye, pink, and chum salmon—plus

steelhead trout—spawn in the coastal streams, providing important resources for both people and a host of wildlife species. Because of the biological productivity of this watershed complex, it is a significant subsistence area for the Native village of Kake, 15 miles to the north.

CLEVELAND PENINSULA

Farther south and east along the southern mainland coast, the Cleveland Peninsula juts into Clarence Strait between Etolin and Revillagigedo islands, north of Ketchikan. The Cleveland is unusual on the mainland

Elisabeth "Sissi" Babich ~ Juneau

". . . we need the forest for the fish."

In 1973 at age 22, Sissi Babich left her small mountain home in the Austrian Alps and set out for the fishing town of Gig Harbor, Washington. En route, she met a sixth-generation fisherman who would eventually become her husband. Her life has been intertwined with fishing ever since.

She started out building and operating a seine boat with her husband, fishing in Alaska in the summer and returning to Washington in the winter. She eventually moved to Southeast Alaska and ran a gill net boat on her own as one of only a few women operators in the area at the time. Fishing allowed her to be her own boss in a setting she loved.

"When you're out there in your boat, you're constantly scanning the horizon and watching the weather," says Babich. "You watch the color of the water, the seagulls, and the other boats casting nets and moving around. It's nonstop observing and making decisions based on your observations."

Babich was quick to learn and adapt to changing conditions in the marketplace. In the late 1980s and early 1990s, the price for wild salmon dropped because of an influx of cheap farm-raised salmon. With decreased demand, it was no longer profitable to sell her catch to a middleman, and so she began to market her fish directly to high-end restaurants in Seattle and other cities. This involved cultivating clients and taking the utmost care with the fish at every step of the process in order to deliver a quality product. Her hard work

paid off, and she turned her attention to an even more specialized seafood market.

"We kept throwing the roe overboard when we cleaned the fish, but I knew that salmon caviar was being sold in specialty stores in Europe," she says.

So in 1993, Babich and several partners started Northern Keta, a salmon caviar business based in Juneau. In keeping with Babich's philosophy of delivering the highest quality, the company prepares roe in the "ancient way"—processed by hand and soaked in brine to produce delicate caviar with the consistency of honey. Babich, known around town as the "egg lady," describes her caviar as wild and a cut above organic—pure, natural, and fresh, just as nature intended.

Nationwide, more people are concerned about where their food comes from and how it's produced, and the health benefits of eating wild salmon are well documented. In addition, the Alaska salmon fishery has been certified by the Marine Stewardship Council, the world's leading certification program for sustainable seafood. Babich's company is a certified supplier of Alaska salmon products.

"If you want to do something good for your family, then buy wild salmon because it's unadulterated," she says. "There are lots of variables that make our salmon healthy and one of them is a healthy forest. We are the last place left on Earth that has abundant wild salmon, and we need the forest for the fish," she says.

ABOVE Petersburg Harbor

coast because it sustains productive forests with relatively large trees. These forests provide good winter deer habitat and support the highest deer densities on the mainland coast. Both black and brown bears inhabit the Cleveland as well as mountain goats and wolves. Twenty-five years ago during a helicopter survey of mountain goats, I observed scattered bands of goats on open ridges at tree line, and I remember being struck by the vastness of this forested peninsula and its unbroken tracts of old growth.

The Cleveland also has abundant salmon-spawning and -rearing habitat, and all five Pacific salmon species, plus steelhead, spawn on the peninsula. Watersheds of particular note here include Union Bay, Port Stewart (especially distinguished for its large estuary), Helm Bay, Yes Bay (with high habitat values for bears, marbled murrelets, and king and sockeye salmon), Spacious Bay (with excellent bear, deer, steelhead, coho, and pink salmon habitat), and Vixen Inlet (with quality bear and chum salmon habitat). The peninsula is also an important recreation and subsistence area for the city of Ketchikan.

Although the surrounding landscape has a substantial history of logging, the Cleveland is still largely intact and provides an outstanding opportunity for landscape-scale conservation. The long-term conservation of ecological values on the southern mainland coast will largely be determined by future management decisions for the Cleveland Peninsula.

HONKER DIVIDE

Prince of Wales Island, in the southern portion of the Alexander Archipelago, west of Ketchikan, is the largest island in the Tongass National Forest. The North Prince of Wales Province (encompassing 80 percent of the island)

is the top-ranked Tongass province for overall ecological values. It has the highest proportion of large-tree forest, winter deer habitat, summer black bear habitat, and more miles of salmon streams than any other Tongass province. The Prince of Wales complex is also a center for endemic populations in Southeast Alaska, including the wolf, flying squirrel, ermine, and spruce grouse. Because of its highly productive lands, this province also has the highest logging activity and road network in the Tongass.

Honker Divide, located on east Prince of Wales between Thorne Bay and Whale Pass, is the largest undeveloped area in the province. This watershed complex—consisting of South Honker, Center Peak, and North Honker watersheds—provides a critical ecological link between the Karta River Wilderness to the south and Sarkar Lake to the north, both of which are intact watersheds with high habitat values in their own right—making the Honker complex unique. Watersheds within the Honker Divide rank among the province's top 10 percent (out of 117 watersheds) for black bear and Sitka black-tailed deer habitat and within the top 5 percent for coho, sockeye, chum, and pink salmon habitat.

When I surveyed Prince of Wales from a small floatplane, Honker Divide stood out as an island oasis of natural habitat surrounded by a sea of clear-cuts, second growth, and roads. This core area is particularly important for maintaining the Prince of Wales wolf population, which is put at risk because of the area's high road density. According to state wildlife biologists, Honker Divide may prove to be an essential component for maintaining the ecological integrity of the most biologically productive province in the entire Tongass—and the province with the most intensive development history and smallest proportion of watershed-scale reserves.

RIGHT Honker Lake (also known as Lake Galea) in the Honker Divide watershed on Prince of Wales Island. Honker Divide is a critical wildlife corridor, particularly for wolves, linking the Karta River Wilderness to the south and Sarkar Lake to the north.

ABOVE During the first weeks of its life, a deer fawn's best defense against predators is to lie motionless in thick vegetation.

RIGHT Forest and muskeg on Admiralty Island

and
trees
in the
salmon

Southeast, panhandle,
Tongass, Inside Passage—
by any name, this place
is where everything flows
into everything else.

DOUGLAS H. CHADWICK

an Johnson looked out over Chatham Strait in Southeast Alaska, where the salmon, whales, and currents swirl while tides of clouds cover and uncover the peaks beyond and you never know what might appear next. "We were standing around by the houses when a huge bear loped past us," he said. "It went down the hillside right toward where Martha Nelson was walking. As it got close, we lost sight of her behind its body, this bear was so big."

Johnson is a tribal leader in Angoon, a Tlingit village of about four hundred residents on Admiralty Island. Martha Nelson is one of the community's Elders, small and getting well on in years. As for the bear, it was *Ursus arctos,* generally known along the coast as the brown bear, or brownie, and elsewhere as the grizzly.

"We ran to help, worried like crazy," Johnson continued. "Instead, we find this little old lady standing there yelling at the bear and shaking

her finger in its face. Man, she's reading it the riot act. And that bear just sort of sags down and hangs its head, like it's ashamed. 'Martha,' we asked after it left, 'what did you say to that animal?'"

Seventeen-hundred-square-mile Admiralty Island —called *Kootznoowoo* in Tlingit, "Fortress of the Bears"— holds an astonishing 1700 brownies, no two with quite the same temperament. Whatever else Martha Nelson called her visitor, she probably addressed it by the traditional title of Grandfather. The Tlingit have always considered other creatures as powerful clans with languages, customs, and thoughts of their own. This sense of kinship becomes easier to grasp in Southeast Alaska among record densities of bears, both black and brown; humpback whales, orcas, and Dall's porpoises, all with large brains and cooperative feeding strategies; wolf families, industrious beavers, palavering ravens, trumpeting swans, sociable sea lions, and rafts of sea otters, which often carry around a favorite rock tool for cracking open urchins and clams.

Many refer to Southeast as the state's panhandle. Others call it the Tongass, since almost 80 percent of

PREVIOUS PAGE Fish Creek on Douglas Island

ABOVE Pack Creek estuary on Admiralty Island

ABOVE Brown bear
eating nutritious sedges in
the Pack Creek estuary

the countryside is the Tongass National Forest. Looking inside, the scientist might say: national rain forest. The spirit, beholding a roof of evergreen sweet as incense raised 150 feet skyward on pillars 20 to 25 feet around, whispers: national house of prayer. Among the richest, most complex natural communities studied, old-growth temperate rain forests harbor an impressive diversity of species and can actually store more organic material per acre than tropical rain forests do. So much of the total biomass is carbon that some experts view cool rain forests as invaluable allies in the current struggle to prevent runaway climate change. Such forests used to fringe many countries, from Japan to Norway to New Zealand. Most have fallen to the ax. At 16.8 million acres, the Tongass is three times the size of the next largest U.S. national forest. In fact, it's larger than nine U.S. states and several entire nations—and it harbors nearly a third of the old-growth temperate rain forest left on Earth.

Geographically, the Tongass consists of a long strip of the mainland, with its soaring coastal mountain range and crag-dwelling white goats, plus a dozen large islands such as Admiralty, at least a thousand smaller islands,

ABOVE Dawes Glacier
in Tracy Arm-Fords Terror
Wilderness

and still thousands more islets and partially exposed reefs—the Alexander Archipelago. Mariners know the sheltered route between these islands and the coast as the northern part of the Inside Passage. Glacier Bay National Park and Preserve adds another 3.3 million acres to the region. Rivers and streams contribute 13,750 miles of tumbling silver. And there's the 18,000 miles of shoreline—more than the forty-eight contiguous states can claim all together—and all the fjords, channels, bays, inlets, and sounds in between.

That the Tongass is among the planet's loveliest settings as well as one of its outstanding biological hot spots is no accident. The dramatic ice-cut topography and beckoning marine passageways both drive dynamic

RIGHT Trumpeter swans
(*Cygnus buccinator*)

processes that yield life in profusion. Beyond that, the landscapes and seascapes interact in ways that multiply each other's vitality. The result? A superecosystem.

As federal domain, the great majority of Tongass lands and resources are owned by the American public. In the national forest portion, much is also available for commercial and industrial use. In particular, the old-growth timber has been heavily exploited in some areas. Any number of battles between development and conservation interests continue today. K. J. Metcalf, a former leader of the Tongass National Forest planning team, recently told me, "Officials hear plenty from special interests and politicians. They don't hear enough from regular citizens. Part of the problem is that an awful lot of Americans don't know that this place exists. You ask folks from outside Alaska what the Tongass is, you get a lot of shrugs. If you say it's one of the world's great rain forests, they think it must be somewhere like Brazil."

To keep this superecosystem from going to pieces under twenty-first-century pressures, the obvious first step is for more folks to become aware of it. And, no, the next step is not for them to start worrying about how to protect the Tongass. The next step is simply to pause and celebrate the place. This book was made to introduce the region and pass along the joys of discovering its special wild and human dimensions. Once readers are better acquainted with such a realm, the sense of responsibility for its future well-being will come.

Southeast, panhandle, Tongass, Inside Passage—by any name, this place is where everything flows into everything else. Hundreds of inches of rain fall every year, growing spire after tower of western redcedar, yellow-

LEFT Clocked at speeds of 30 knots, the Dall's porpoise (*Phocoenoides dalli*) may be the fastest of all the small cetaceans. At high speeds, the animal's head and back produce a "rooster tail," which creates a hollow cone allowing the animal to breathe underwater.

CLOCKWISE FROM TOP LEFT Anemone and social tunicates in Chatham Strait • China rockfish (*Sebastes nebulosus*) among cold water gorgonian corals in Suloia Bay • Nudibranchs, the "slugs of the sea," in Chatham Strait

cedar, western hemlock, and Sitka spruce. Some of the elders reach a thousand years of age. Dominating most slopes, the conifers become scaffolding for a vast aerial collection of ferns, liverworts, mosses, and shelf fungi. These epiphytes build pockets of soil that gradually sift down onto the ground. Hundreds of different lichens coat the trees as well. A few contain nitrogen-fixing bacteria and drip this vital building block of proteinlike fertilizer each time it rains.

Beneath the conifers spreads a second canopy of salmonberry, blueberry, and other shrubs. Below them, ferns and wildflowers cover a forest floor that is merely

the ceiling for more tiers of life—a springy, sprawling, composting heap of fallen debris several feet thick. It houses nations of little beasts from millipedes and mites to nematode worms. The roots down in this crowded basement attach to an array of symbiotic fungi, which bring the plants minerals and other nutrients from microniches in return for a little starch. Miles of these invisible mold filaments, called mycorrhizae, crisscross every handful of forest-floor duff, fashioning a literal web of life that boosts the health and vigor of the green mansions above.

The heavy precipitation also feeds massive

ABOVE Thorne River in the Honker Divide watershed on Prince of Wales Island

glaciers that rasp the mountainsides with such force that the blue ice never flows over quite the same contours twice. Rocks and soils with biologically essential elements such as iron get carried along all the way from the summits to the tides. Smaller glaciers and snowfields melt into streams that cascade through tundra, muskeg, and then the rain-forest communities, gathering silt and organic compounds at every stage. Eventually, the waterways deposit this material in shallow, fan-shaped estuaries. More than ten thousand pattern the Tongass, supporting pastures of sedges and head-high grasses in the upper part of the deltas, as well as sea-grass nurseries for young fish toward the outer reaches.

UPPER RIGHT Found in muskegs and wet meadows, the round-leaf sundew (*Drosera rotundifolia*) is a carnivorous plant that catches insects with its sticky glandular tentacles.

LOWER RIGHT Stink currant (*Ribes bracteosum*) produces large clumps of currants that are an important food source for bears.

Just offshore, another great forest begins. Like the conifer woodlands, its biomass per acre ranks among the highest measured. But this northern jungle is made of kelp. At low tide, the seaweed drapes over rock walls like vines claiming the ruins of a temple. When the tide comes in, however, the forest floats free. To enter it with diving gear is to slowly fly through the softest thickets imaginable. Fronds of bull kelp, *Laminaria,* and feather boa ripple with the currents and flex with the waves, and each time they move, new constellations of purple sea stars and flame-colored sponges peek through. Though the kelp strands are slippery, divers can get tangled up now and then, suspended in another web of life while schools of young herring, ling cod, or baby salmon dazzle past like sunlit streaks of rain. Together with estuaries, the kelp forests are key habitats in the life cycles of many fish, offering juveniles too small to take their chances in open water, shelter from predators and storms.

Uncertainty comes with the scenery here. Williwaw gusts can broadside you around a corner, while seal-speckled icebergs barge out of the fjords. Narrows smooth as whale skin during slack tide morph into rapids and waterfalls during the outflow. Yet the tremendous energies coursing through this system are part of what make it so fecund. The stronger the currents in a given area, the faster they deliver nutrients and oxygen, and the more prolific the intertidal community will be.

In the broadest sense, nearly the whole of Southeast qualifies as one grand estuary. Scientists can track its plume of sediments, nutrients, and freshwater all the way north through the Gulf of Alaska to the Bering Sea. Everything flows into everything else. It flows down, and it flows out. And then it flows back up the streams and the slopes again.

From the ocean's edge into the rain forest, the day gives way to a damp twilight full of deeper shadows. Whatever is not green and gloaming is woody brown. The wind has gone with the sky. In place of the rolling hiss and thrum of the sea, there is overwhelming stillness, a hush so pervasive that the place seems about to speak its name. Yet there are crab shells and the cracked husks of urchins on that mossy trampoline of a forest floor. The nutrients are starting their return journey

LEFT The commercial salmon fishery is a mainstay of the economy of Southeast Alaska, and the state's salmon fishery has been certified as sustainable.

ABOVE Bonaparte gulls (*Larus philadelphia*) diving for salmon eggs

inland with the help of foraging ravens, bald eagles, gulls, and the mammals that etch the woodland trails paralleling the shore.

Black-tailed deer emerge from the boughs to graze the beaches and estuary meadows through the warm months. During tough winters, they can always find kelp to eat at low tide. Bears gravitate from their dens each spring to the estuaries and graze the first new sprouts beside the deer. The bears also dig for clams, munch mussels, turn over rocks for shore crabs, and even lick up snails and pillbug-size marine isopods.

After leaving the rivers and the estuaries where they lingered as smolts, the region's iconic salmon school across the Pacific, gaining weight and strength. When they return years later to spawn in the freshwater where they were born, many keep thrashing toward the summits until an unleapable waterfall blocks the way. All five species of Pacific salmon breed in the Tongass, each packing a collection of nitrogen and carbon from the marine realm up the slopes. Steelhead, sea-run cutthroat trout, and the char known as Dolly Varden migrate between the salt- and freshwater as well.

Racing, swatting, belly-flopping bears catch dozens of salmon per day during runs. Coastal wolves—those of the archipelago are a unique subspecies—do more fishing than anyone used to suspect. Smaller hunters, from mink to marten, carry salmon into the woods to eat, leaving more carcasses strewn about, together with urine and dung. Bald eagles and ravens do the same. Harlequin ducks dive to raid the fishes' gravel nests. Even Steller's jays, normally found high in the conifers, wade in after loose eggs. Chickadees peck at leftover fish. I've seen deer nibbling carcasses, too, probably treating them like a transitory mineral lick.

Fish scale by dung pile by molted feather by moldering bone—the riches spread out from the water courses onto the mountainsides. Trees near salmon streams grow faster and larger than those farther away. The same is true for bushes, and they produce more berries and seeds. Salmon bodies sunk in the channels or decaying along banks nourish extra plankton and aquatic insect larvae, which feed the next generation of fry. Other carcasses bump downstream to wash up on estuary shores, where they add to the natural wealth banked in the delta silts.

~~~~~

It's one thing to intellectually grasp the importance of nutrient cycles and connections within ecosystems. It's another to touch them directly. That's not only possible here in the Tongass, it's hard to avoid. Once you sense salmon in the trees, you begin to see the rain forest's chemistry in the salmon, and in the crabs and kelp. You can visualize that the wolves trotting off with fish are helping grow the berries that bears eat. You feel tidal rips, where fish gather to feed, surging in the wing flaps of eagles. Residues of glacial ice in the cruising orca pods. Clouds in the salmon, and salmon in the Tlingit and their language, which has no word for starvation. Everything flowing into everything else. This isn't New Age rhapsodizing. It's what the ages have wrought.

"I went fishing for sockeye up in Mitchell Bay the other day," said Jamie Daniels, a resident of Angoon, "and I was thanking those salmon I caught. Their ancestors fed my ancestors. I told the fish I would always be grateful."

Tlingit territory was potlatch country; people gained status not by the amount of food and goods they hoarded but by how much they gave away at great feasts. It was a measure of the generosity of the sea and slopes that enfolded them. Not every aspect of life was idyllic; warfare and the taking of women and slaves during raids were common practices. But the Tlingit never diminished the natural resources that sustained their culture, and it prospered generation after generation. At her Angoon home, artist JoAnn George showed me a sharp-ended stick from nearby Favorite Bay. Her husband had tripped over it while hunting deer on the tidal flats. He pulled at the thing, expecting a waterlogged branch to emerge from the muck. It was a stake from a fish trap later dated at three thousand years of age.

In the eighteenth century, a culture that viewed nature as inferior and wild flora and fauna as commodities sailed in. The invaders—Russians, then Americans of European descent—came to plunder hides and fur. Next, it was gold, and then oil from whales until that played out. Teddy Roosevelt established the Tongass National Forest in 1907, but it remained open to exploitation. Within a few years, shoreline logging was already making true goliaths among the conifers scarce. Some politicians lobbied to exterminate brown bears, arguing that they posed an obstacle to expanding the timber industry.

The outlook for *Ursus arctos* improved during the 1930s as Alaska developed plans for bear management. But the plan for the rain forest was to convert it into a vast plantation for wood, eliminating virtually all old

RIGHT The Native cultures in the Tongass region have endured for thousands of years.

Barry Bracken ~ Petersburg

"... the greatest value of this ecosystem is maintaining it as close to its natural existence as possible."

Outside Barry Bracken's living-room window, humpback whales, fishing boats, and kayaks cruise the waters of Frederick Sound. Sitka black-tailed deer browse the intertidal plants in his beachfront yard. And on rare occasions, the ever-present low clouds rise to reveal Devils Thumb, a jagged Coast Range mountain on the border of Alaska and British Columbia.

"What's not to like?" says Bracken. "Southeast Alaska is one of the last accessible places in the world where both the marine and land environments still pretty much remain in a wild state. It's very difficult, if not impossible, to separate them as there's so much interconnectedness."

A marine biologist, Bracken spent twenty-three years with the Alaska Department of Fish and Game. In the early 1970s, he was part of a multidisciplinary team studying aspects of forest ecology, including fisheries, soils, fungi, and wildlife. He experienced many areas of the Tongass in their unaltered states and gained an understanding of the complexity of the region's watersheds. From bears and other animals dragging salmon carcasses and associated marine nutrients into the forest, to the streamside vegetation shading and nurturing the salmon spawning grounds, Bracken and others found that the Tongass needs all of its ecological parts in order to function.

"This is a remarkable system that works because it has been largely left intact, even though there are places that have been decimated," he says. "I don't think people appreciate just how fragile the whole system is, though. Some people don't care, and others feel technology will take care of it. But it needs to be left intact for all the parts to work together."

To help people understand and actually experience the connections in the Tongass, Bracken started Kaleidoscope Cruises after retiring from the Department of Fish and Game in 1995. He takes small groups of people on whale-watching and glacier tours aboard his boat *Island Dream*. Bracken, now 60, also gives presentations on the area's ecology in his hometown of Petersburg.

Even for those who may never visit the Tongass, simply knowing that such a large, intact ecosystem exists has intrinsic value to the collective psyche of the American people, according to Bracken. He feels that preserving special places like the Tongass and forgoing our economic self-interests speak volumes about who we are as a nation.

"My hope is that people will come to the realization that the greatest value of this ecosystem is maintaining it as close to its natural existence as possible," he says. "We need to look forward and maintain an economic balance and the fragile ecology of the area. If there's a chance of doing this anywhere in the world, I think we can do it here."

ABOVE The arched back of the humpback whale earned it its common name.

growth. In 1947, this started to turn into a reality when Congress passed the Tongass Timber Act, which guaranteed companies willing to build pulp mills a fifty-year supply of national forest trees at token prices.

Why not? When it came to natural resources, post–World War II America was thinking with a different vocabulary. Ecology was a brand new science, and few had even heard the term. The watchword was progress, defined as ever-increasing industrial activity. Forest managers labeled old growth as stagnant, decadent,

ABOVE Black bear fishing at Dog Salmon Creek on Prince of Wales Island

overmature, senile, even sterile. The healthiest woodlands with the best food for wildlife, they assured folks, were those in the stages of regrowth. One enormous pulp mill went up in Sitka, another in Ketchikan, and five-hundred-year-old spruce and hemlock elders fed their insatiable appetites.

A 1971 act of Congress, intended to give indigenous Alaskans control over resources they had always relied upon, let Native regional and village corporations choose 44 million acres within the state for their own purposes. But the Native corporations in Southeast didn't necessarily select traditional hunting and fishing territories. Advised by economists and lobbyists, most picked old-growth strongholds and promptly set about leveling them, doubling the total amount of timber cut in Southeast to more than a billion board feet some years.

The pulp industry provided steady employment and significant income for mill workers, loggers, truckers, and various communities. On the other hand, the big mills drove independent small operators out of business. Air and water pollution around the pulp factories grew to health-threatening levels. Prince of Wales, the southernmost of the large Tongass islands, started to look like the scalped, road-webbed forestlands of western Oregon or Washington. Since the mills paid next to nothing for the trees, whereas the costs of building roads and laying out timber sales were steep, the Tongass lost far more money than any other national forest every year. U.S. taxpayers made up the difference, though most never realized it.

Then the U.S. Forest Service proposed logging pristine Admiralty Island to supply a third pulp mill. Opposition from conservationists, sportsmen, commercial fishermen, and Native people, notably the Angoon community, stiffened. Lawsuits were filed. Publicity about heavily subsidized logging in this hinterland spread in the Lower 48. During 1978, President Jimmy Carter declared nearly the whole of the island a national monument and also proclaimed 2.3 million acres on the mainland as Misty Fiords National Monument. Two years later fourteen new wilderness areas were established in the Tongass, while Glacier Bay

National Monument was expanded to become Glacier Bay National Park and Preserve, raising the total area protected in Southeast Alaska to 8.7 million acres.

Nevertheless, an unsustainable volume of old growth continued pouring into the two mills in Sitka and Ketchikan. Congress revised the original Tongass Timber Act, lowering the allowable cut in order to comply with newer standards for protecting wildlife and watersheds. The reform was a partial success—until Alaska politicians maneuvered to raise the quota again. What *was* the highest and best use of this public domain? To create more jobs for remote communities? To protect water quality and fisheries? To safeguard wildlife habitats for Native subsistence? For tourism? Despite the many kinds of resources bound together within the Tongass ecosystem, the arguments always seemed to come back to the single issue of timber. Many wondered if the timber controversy would ever end before the last giant vanished. Some still wonder today.

~~~

Opinions are important. Facts should count for more. Here are the central ones: While plenty of the Tongass qualifies as temperate rain forest, much of that consists of small to modest-size trees rooted in poorly drained, boggy ground or cold subalpine terrain. Roughly 40 percent of this national forest is completely unforested, covered with rocks, ice, snow, alpine, muskeg, or avalanche slopes instead. The big-tree old growth—which keeps attracting saws, winch cables, and bulldozer blades like a magnetic force—makes up less than 3 percent of the land base.

True, younger trees grow more quickly and may be managed like crops to yield more board feet of wood per acre. But old-growth forests generate the greatest

abundance and diversity of life. Antiquity is their prime. They, not successional stands, provide the most reliable food for animals. When huge trees die naturally and topple over, they create light gaps—openings that fill with edible vegetation. Like spawned-out salmon around streams, the elders then contribute the nutrients from their own decaying bodies, boosting new growth.

True, clear-cutting also provides a lot of forage for wildlife as herbs, shrubs, and saplings come roaring back among sunstruck stumps. Before long, though, the brush is so thick that animals begin to have trouble moving through it. And that isn't the main problem. Winter is. During the coldest, toughest months, that vegetation is buried under a deep snowpack, unavailable when animals need it the most. By contrast, falling snow gets intercepted by the tall branches of old-growth stands. The creatures below enjoy ready shelter, easier traveling, and more access to food. Ask the bears. Ask the deer.

ABOVE More than one hundred public recreation cabins allow local residents and visitors to experience the wilds of the Tongass National Forest.

RIGHT Every year, more than 350,000 people visit the Mendenhall Glacier in the Tongass National Forest. Mendenhall is part of the Juneau Icefield, North America's fifth largest icefield covering 1500 square miles and feeding thirty-eight large glaciers.

Studies have proved that they and many smaller species strongly prefer the ancient forests much of the year.

As regrowth continues in logged areas, the situation gets worse. Most sites end up monopolized by phalanxes of hemlock or spruce packed so tightly that direct light does not reach the forest floor. So little grows there that the animals might as well have bare pavement under their feet, and the habitat can remain in this condition for a century. In short, clear-cutting in temperate rain forests leads to a lengthy stage of nearly

LEFT Fly fishing the Thorne River on Prince of Wales Island

RIGHT Members of the woodpecker family, red-breasted sapsuckers (*Sphyrapicus ruber*) depend on dead snags and trees with heart rot for drumming, nesting, roosting, and feeding sites.

sterile woodland, the very thing forest managers claimed old growth to be. The trees come back, but minus the beauty, enchantment, and natural wealth and variety of life found where the elders still reign.

Before settlement, North America's temperate rain forest extended along the Pacific Coast from Alaska to northern California. The majority has since been logged and highly fragmented from central British Columbia south. In fact, 96 percent of old-growth woodlands of every kind, from Louisiana cypress to California oak, have been cut across southern Canada and the Lower 48. The Tongass harbors by far the greatest concentration of big trees in the United States, even after losing between a third and a half of them to the saws.

Toward the close of the twentieth century, the international market for pulp grew weaker. Countries in warmer, less remote parts of the world could provide fiber and lumber more cheaply than Alaska. On top of everything else, the Tongass timber corporations were facing serious fines for pollution and lawsuits from residents blaming the toxins for serious illnesses. In 1997, the last big Tongass mill shut down.

Progress has taken on different meanings in the twenty-first century. Tourism, particularly the cruise ship industry, is now a dominant player in the economy. It revitalized Sitka and Ketchikan and bolstered commerce in Juneau, the main population center in sparsely inhabited Southeast Alaska. Visitors come to experience glaciers, grizzlies, whales, and untamed vistas. They're looking for a break from the relentlessly busier and more crowded modern world, not for another frontier being cut down to size. The sport-fishing business has become as valuable as the commercial fishing industry, and neither group wants to see one more spawning stream degraded by logging and erosion.

Only a couple of medium-size mills and a scattering of small ones still operate. They process a fraction of the amount of timber formerly cut. But the quantity versus quality value system has been turned on its head. A gigantic spruce that used to sell as a raw log for the price of a cheeseburger is worth tens of thousands of dollars if hand-milled into "music wood"—planks whose exceptionally strong, evenly spaced fibers make ideal sounding boards for string instruments. Big cedars that the pulp industry considered trash have become the most valuable trees. Asian craftsmen especially treasure the lustrous grain of old-growth yellow-cedar for sculptures and veneer. They could perhaps relate to the Native tradition of cutting one cedar plank or root at a time from a living tree, leaving the titan to heal and continue its role within the forest community.

At the simplest yet deepest level, we're all after the same things as the wild species: dependable food, shelter, and security. Yet humans also need hope and inspiration. There are more than enough of those qualities in the Tongass to go around, for residents and swelling numbers of visitors alike. It's the nature of this region to provide in abundance. Rather than stay fixated

LEFT Nootka lupine
(*Lupinus nootkatensis*)
along Lynn Canal

RIGHT Picking wild blue-
berries in the rain forest

on points of disagreement, we might think about what a blessing it is to have such extraordinary natural wealth to argue over. Maybe the goal should be agreeing on ways to go with its flow.

"We have an ecosystem that's taken a lot of hits," ecologist John Sisk told me, "but it's still fundamentally intact. I can't imagine a place with a better opportunity to come up with a new ecosystem management strategy and new ways of people working together." Proposals for lumbering and road building in primeval forests continue to be the chief source of contention. Going after the largest conifers still makes the most economic sense for timbermen. But it remains equally true that the big

trees help create many of the loveliest, most biologically diverse and productive sites in the landscape. To other people and all kinds of other life forms, those wild strongholds are simply priceless.

Applying advanced computer technology to the best available field data, scientists with Audubon Alaska and The Nature Conservancy have created maps of big-tree old growth, salmon streams, estuaries, deer wintering sites, nesting areas for the declining seabirds known as marbled murrelets, which fly miles inland to nest in ancient forests, and other key biological elements. The watersheds where these overlap are the crucial organs of the living system that is the Tongass,

Where the Forest Meets the Sea

AMY GULICK

Hunched over my tripod on a muddy tidal flat, I look through the viewfinder at a giant set of fresh grizzly bear tracks. I fire off a few shots and then recompose for a different angle. Before tripping the shutter, I check the viewfinder one last time and see water inching into the frame. I look down and my feet are submerged. The tide has arrived. *This* is why rubber boots are an essential part of every Southeast Alaskan's wardrobe.

I'm standing in the wide mouth of a stream where it empties into a protected coastal bay. A place like this, called an estuary, is in a constant state of flux as the tides ebb and flow, mixing the stream's freshwater and the ocean's saltwater. Rich with nutrients and salt-tolerant plants, an estuary is a biological buffet. The bear that left the now-flooded tracks I just photographed was likely dining on a fresh salad of sedges. Estuaries are magnets for bears and other wildlife that come for the smorgasbord of plants, clams, bugs, and spawning salmon headed for their birth streams. People come too, gathering seaweed, gumboot chitons, and goosetongue plants at low tide. And it's not unusual to trip over thousand-year-old wooden stakes poking out of streambanks and tidal flats—remnants of fish traps ingeniously crafted by the Tlingit people.

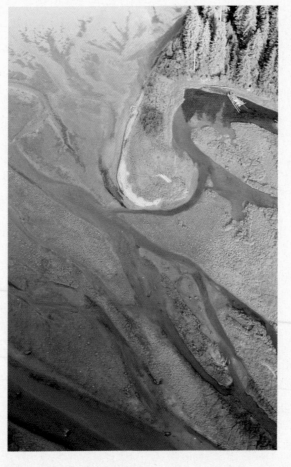

As the tide chases me farther inland, I splash through the shallow channels. Young flounders and sculpins dart away from my boots. I tiptoe around orange and purple sea stars that don't have the luxury of fleeing. Stepping onto dry ground, I merge onto a bear freeway—a well-worn trail where the big furry critters have matted down the chest-high vegetation. "Hello bears," I call out. "I mean you no harm." I gingerly make my way through a profusion of wildflowers—red Indian paintbrush, chocolate lilies, and dainty shooting stars. At the edge of the forest, I duck under a Sitka spruce branch and enter a different world. Gone is the sticky smell of salt spray, traded for the earthy aroma of wet wood. Gone is the bright light of open sky, replaced by a luxuriant canopy of green. Not gone is the bear freeway, and I continue talking to the unseen bruins as I pick my way through prickly devil's club and scooch over fallen trees.

After a couple of miles of slogging through a riot of green and tangle of trees, my brain is hundreds of miles away from any thought of the ocean. I stop to rest and at my feet, on a carpet of moss, are barnacle-covered mussel shells. An otter or raven likely carried them inland, a reminder that deep in the forests of the Tongass, the sea is never far away.

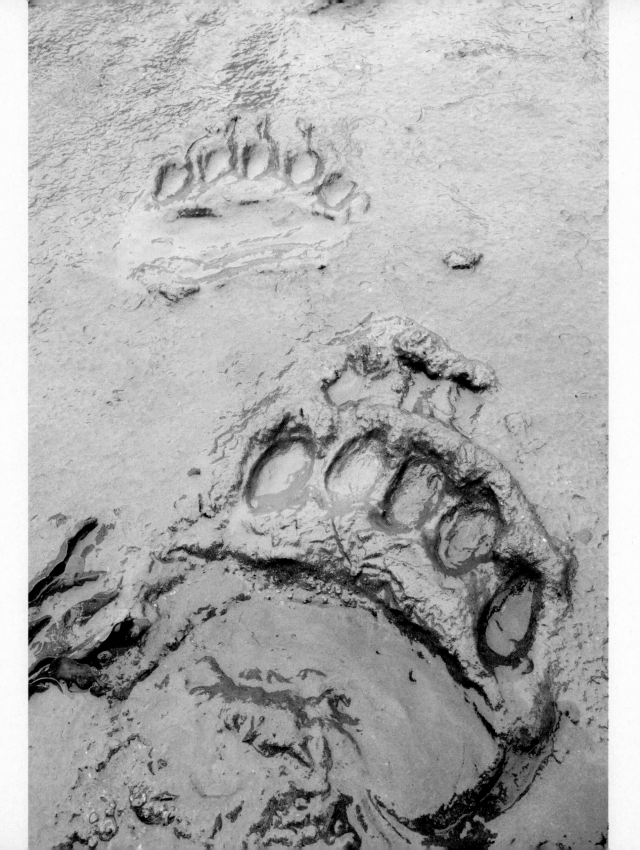

LEFT Shallow, fan-shaped estuaries are places where freshwater streams and ocean tides mix.

RIGHT Brown bear tracks in an estuary on Admiralty Island

and, thus, the premier candidates for protection. At the same time, conservationists are working to identify areas where the timber industry could obtain a dependable supply of trees, perhaps by thinning closed-in stands of hemlock in previously logged areas.

Among other concerns in the region is the decline of fisheries, notably salmon, halibut, and the herring that used to sweep through like living tides and leave shorelines swamped with their glistening eggs. Overfishing is partly to blame. But oceanic conditions may be affecting the populations as well, which brings up the challenge of climate change. When Captain George Vancouver sailed through Icy Strait in 1794, there was no Glacier Bay, only the glacier that filled it. Cruise ships now travel 65 miles inland through open waters to see that glacier's tongue crumbling into a fjord. In the meantime, Native issues, mining operations, and potential impacts from tourism and recreation need attention. All kinds of decisions affecting the region's lands and waters lie ahead. Who's going to make them?

~~~~~

Starting in 1978, K. J. Metcalf was the monument ranger for newly protected Admiralty Island. Discouraged that the Forest Service's priorities stayed skewed toward

ABOVE Brown bear sow and cub take a break from salmon fishing on Admiralty Island.

harvesting timber, K. J. finally quit and went on to run the general store in Angoon for the next eighteen years with his wife Peggy. The Tlingit adopted him into the tribe's Killer Whale Clan. One day, he and I paddled a canoe from Angoon into Mitchell Bay. The mix of flows from the oceans and mountains makes this complex of lakes and inlets one of the world's foremost subsistence areas. Salmon, crabs, and gumboot chitons wait in the shallows.

Geese and ducks drift over them. On the islets, rocky points bulge with resting harbor seals. Ashore, otters trot from cockle to mussel, and bears amble among edible goosetongue and chocolate lilies, whose bulbs produce starchy outgrowths known as Indian rice.

On a flood tide, K. J. and I were able to ease through passages no wider than creeks into a hidden bay the Tlingit call Baby Pouch, ringed by gentle hills and forests.

LEFT Just offshore from the rain forest, underwater kelp forests are home to a diversity of marine life.

CLOCKWISE FROM TOP LEFT Red columbine (*Aquilegia formosa*) • Northern rice root (*Fritillaria camschatcensis*) • Oak fern (*Gymnocarpium dryopteris*) and false lily-of-the-valley (*Maianthemum dilatatum*) • Shooting star (*Dodecatheon pulchellum*)

The breeze faded. The air became warm and close. The water's glassy surface doubled the sky. We seemed to be gliding on soft rain clouds that rippled in our wake. Ravens carried on distant conversations, grawking and gabbling yet sometimes issuing calls that tolled like purely struck bells. Loons cruised ahead, acting as escort vessels to show us the way, except that I no longer wanted to go anywhere. Swaddled in the tranquility of Baby Pouch, I closed my eyes and nodded off toward sleep.

Before dreams took over, I thought how curious it is that students can graduate from a U.S. high school knowing obscure facts about bygone kingdoms yet almost nothing about the third of their own nation that is public domain. It's as if a relative died and willed them an inconceivably vast estate full of treasure, but no one made an effort to tell them about it.

Americans have been given many gifts and none greater than this empire beyond anything the wealthiest individual could ever possess. By dint of simple citizenship, I own part of the Shenandoah Valley, the rolling Great Plains, and coral reefs off the Florida Keys. And that's only a small sample of my holdings. They also include the immensities of Southeast. Alaskans aren't the only ones who should chart its future. Whether we live in Arizona or New Jersey, we hold equal title to the splendors and freedoms of the Tongass, just as our parents did and our children will after us. By the same token, we are equally responsible for whatever happens there and for directing the agencies that serve as its stewards.

When I woke up, the tide was on the verge of turning. We paddled on, flowing past the old gravesite of a shaman among tall trees bordering the channel. It was the main route toward the backcountry where the sockeye were once again gathering to spawn.

RIGHT Every year, wild salmon leave the ocean and return to their freshwater birth streams to spawn and die.

LEFT In the spring, humpback whales migrate to Alaska where food is abundant, coming primarily from their calving and breeding waters of Hawaii some 2800 miles away.

ABOVE Fairweather Range rises over Icy Strait.

Long may it last:
the big old trees still
standing, the bugs,
the fish, the bears,
and the flawed and
saintly people . . .

ear Ray, Greetings from Sitka, the navel-gazing capital of the north. I think I've told you this before, but I love living in southeast-ern Alaska, and this includes your Ketchikan. I love this forest world in ways that maybe other people don't. It's strange how we accommodate to a place.

There's a joke a friend likes to tell. The Buddha is going to a baseball game and he stops by the hot-dog stand. The vendor asks what he wants on it and the Buddha naturally says, "Make me one with everything."

Or something like that.

What I like about that joke is that he doesn't say, "Make me one with just the beautiful things." He says *everything*. In this place of big trees and fish and some seventy thousand people who live and work in and around the islands of the Tongass, life is wild and also messy. Bugs eat and excrete the trees. Fish rot on the streambanks and the muddy brown

163

rain rinses them out to sea. Shafts of sunlight come down through the ancient forest stands to the stink and decay of life moldering down into the duff. It's butt-ugly in spots and spine-tingling beautiful.

And just like this forest, its people are likewise ugly and fine. Redneck and navel gazer. Island people live by finding life's openings and exploiting those openings until they close back up again. Then we're on to the next. In that way we're not much different from bears or bugs or dying fish. We stink and we look for food and sex, cheeseburgers and salmon steaks. We're omnivorous in all the ways we love this world and want to consume it. We're not saintly, but neither are we dumb or unsophisticated. We're savvy like a black bear on the edge of town, flame-red tongue flicking the sweetness out of this wild and lovely wreckage of a life that is always growing up and falling down.

And that's what I love about living in this huge and contiguous forest. Long may it last: the big old trees still standing, the bugs, the fish, the bears, and the flawed and saintly people who want to live a sensual life in this everything place.

People as strange as you, and your friend,

SALMON: THE FISH THAT DIES FOR LOVE

PREVIOUS PAGE
Mount Edgecumbe,
a long-dormant volcano,
on Kruzof Island

ABOVE *Salmon The Fish That Dies For Love*

RIGHT Commercial fishing
boats at work in Lynn Canal

acknowledgments

It's a common perception that the life of a nature photographer is a solitary one. And while I do spend time alone in the wild, the reality is that this book would not be possible without the help of many incredible people. I'm grateful and humbled by all of their contributions. My best supporter and source of inspiration is my husband Chris, who is always there to listen, carry gear, and share adventures.

Without scientists, the world would not know the connection between salmon and trees, and I would not have been inspired to tell this remarkable story. I am grateful for their important work, and for helping me understand what is often staring me in the face. Special thanks to: Dr. John Schoen (Audubon Alaska); Matt Kirchhoff, Dr. David Person, and Steve McCurdy (Alaska Department of Fish & Game); Jim Baichtal, Terry Fifield, and Katherine Prussian (U.S. Forest Service); Dr. Tom Reimchen (University of Victoria); Scott Gende (National Park Service); Dr. Thomas Quinn (University of Washington); Dr. Mark Wipfli (University of Alaska Fairbanks); and Dr. Paul Alaback (University of Montana).

To the Native Tlingit, Haida, and Tsimshian people who shared themselves and their cultures, I am honored to have been allowed a glimpse into your world. *Gunalchéesh, Háw'aa*, and *'Doyck-shin*: Rosita Worl, Jon Rowan Jr., Noelle Demmert, Jess Isaacs II, Cherilyn and Marilyn Holter, Adrian and Vicki LeCornu, Richard Peterson, Roby and John Littlefield, Teri Rofkar, Tommy Joseph, Mike and Edna Jackson, Diane Douglas-Willard, Paula Varnell, Organized Village of Kake, Chilkat Indian Village of Klukwan, Hydaburg Cooperative Association, Organized Village of Kasaan, Alaska Native Sisterhood Camp #4, and Sealaska Heritage Institute.

Getting around in the Tongass of Southeast Alaska requires serious logistics, boats, and aircraft, and I thank the many skilled captains and pilots for transporting me safely: Michelle Masden (Island Wings), Mike McKimens (Outer Coast Adventures), Brenda Schwartz-Yeager (Alaska Charters and Adventures), Barry Bracken (Kaleidoscope Cruises), Lynn Bennett (L.A.B. Flying), Jeff Wedekind (Chinook Shores), Mike Lever (Nautilus Explorer), Dave Carnes (Legend Charters), Wade Loofbourrow, Scott Harris, and the crews of Ward Air, Alaska Marine Highway System, and Alaska Airlines.

The numerous Alaskans who gave their time to help me are tough, independent, and some of the most gracious people I know, including but not limited to: Michael

ABOVE A garden in Sitka

"Mr. Honker" Kampnich, Scott Ownbey (and dog Ellie), Karen Petersen, Troy and Di Thain, Erica Bjorum, Dave Sherman, Russell Heath, Beth Peluso, Emily Ferry, Rod Cadmus, Mark Gnadt, Butch Carber, Nonna Shtipelman, Tim Bristol, Mark Kaelke, Eric and Amy Jorgensen, Becky Janes, Kaitlyn Bausler, Beth Antonsen, Sissi Babich, K.J. Metcalf, Laurie Cooper, John Sisk, the Jordan Family (Karl, Julie, Lilly, Eva, and Chris), the Harris family (Scott, Patty, and Tommy), Natalie Sattler, Andrew Thoms, Brian McNitt, Dennis Rogers, John "Ace" Yeager, Kathy Bracken, Gordon Chew, Erin Dovichin, Carolyn and Alan Gould, John and Judy Baker, and Gary McWilliams.

I am in awe of the dream team of contributors to this book, each of whom brings the Tongass alive in his or her own talented way: Ray Troll, Richard Nelson, John Straley, Carl Safina, Doug Chadwick, Rosita Worl, Brad Matsen, John Schoen, and Richard Carstensen.

I owe an enormous amount of gratitude to Helen Cherullo, for her trust and patience, and her wonderful team at Braided River: Deb Easter, Kate Rogers, Mary Metz, Margaret Sullivan, Jane Jeszeck, Linda Gunnarson, Julie Van Pelt, Ani Rucki, and Laura Case.

Financial and organizational support were paramount to this project, and my deepest thanks to: Tom and Sonya Campion (Campion Foundation); Dave Secord, Carol Orr, and Tim Greyhavens (Wilburforce Foundation); Don Weeden (Weeden Foundation); Leslie Harroun (Oak Foundation); Sam Skaggs (Skaggs Foundation); The Mountaineers Foundation; North American Nature Photography Association Foundation; CHS Family Charitable Fund; Mark Lukes (Fine Print Imaging); Cindy Shogan (Alaska Wilderness League); Judith Sterry; and Michael Rossotto.

Finally, I am forever grateful to friends and family. My late mother, Alice Selleg, and father Richard Selleg are responsible for my love of nature, art, and adventure. Big thanks to those who provided critical support, editing skills, and enthusiasm throughout the making of this book: Cynthia Wayburn, Liz Wallace, Paul Bannick, Marlyn Twitchell, Steve Kallick, Anne Wilkas, Peter Howland, Heidi King, Robin Werner, Julie Milazzo, Cristina Mittermeier, and Robert Glenn Ketchum.

about the photographer

AMY GULICK is an award-winning nature photographer and writer; she is also a Fellow with the International League of Conservation Photographers. Her images and stories have been featured in *Audubon, National Wildlife, Outdoor Photographer, Nature's Best Photography, Sierra,* and other publications.

Her work in Alaska has received numerous honors including the prestigious Daniel Housberg Wilderness Image Award from the Alaska Conservation Foundation, the Voice of the Wild Award from the Alaska Wilderness League, and a Lowell Thomas Award from the Society of American Travel Writers Foundation. In recognition of her work in the Tongass National Forest, the North American Nature Photography Association Foundation awarded her a Philip Hyde Grant.

Amy grew up in Illinois, spending much of her childhood chasing after frogs and fireflies. Nature photography and writing allow her to continue her pursuits of all things wild. She lives with her husband Chris in the foothills of Washington's Cascade Mountains, sharing their home with bears, bats, and tree frogs.

More of Amy Gulick's work can be seen at www.amygulick.com.

INTERNATIONAL LEAGUE OF
CONSERVATION
PHOTOGRAPHERS

Please also see **www.salmoninthetrees.org** to learn more about Amy's work in the Tongass National Forest.

contributors

RAY TROLL bases his quirky, aquatic images on the latest scientific discoveries, bringing a street-smart sensibility to the worlds of ichthyology and paleontology. After earning his BA from Bethany College in Lindsborg, Kansas in 1977 and an MFA in studio arts from Washington State University in 1981, Troll was awarded an honorary doctorate in fine arts from the University of Alaska Southeast in 2008. He has also received the Alaska Governor's award for the arts and a gold medal for "distinction in the natural history arts" from the Academy of Natural Sciences in Philadelphia. His traveling expeditions have included a "Dancing to the Fossil Record" and "Sharkabet, a Sea of Sharks from A to Z." He has appeared on the Discovery Channel; lectured at Cornell, Harvard, and Yale; shown work at the Smithsonian; and has a ratfish named after him (*Hydrolagus trolli*). He moved to Alaska in 1983 and still lives and works in rain-swept Ketchikan, Alaska. *Photograph by Keith Wadley*

DR. CARL SAFINA brought ocean conservation into the environmental mainstream and is founding president of Blue Ocean Institute. *Audubon* magazine named him among the leading one hundred conservationists of the 20th Century. His hundred-plus publications

and award-winning books include *Song for the Blue Ocean, Eye of the Albatross, Voyage of the Turtle,* and *The View From Lazy Point;* and his writing has been featured in *National Geographic.* He's been profiled by the *New York Times, Nightline,* and Bill Moyers. His awards include a Pew Fellowship, Lannan Literary Award, John Burroughs Medal, and a MacArthur Prize, among others. *Photograph by Patricia Paladines*

RICHARD CARSTENSEN, a naturalist from Juneau, Alaska was one of the founders in the 1980s of Discovery Southeast, a non-profit group bringing natural history education to all of the public schools in Alaska's capital. He is the co-author of *The Nature of Southeast Alaska,* and a contributing writer to *The Enduring Forests, Book of the Tongass,* and *The Coastal Forests and Mountains Ecoregion* (Audubon/TNC). From 1996 to 2004 he was field leader of the Landmark Trees Project, documenting Alaska's finest remaining large-tree forests. In 2005, with Bob Christensen, he began the Ground-Truthing Project, the "eyes and ears in the woods" for the Southeast Alaskan conservation community. *Photograph by Catherine Pohl*

BRAD MATSEN has been writing about the sea and its inhabitants for forty years. He is the author of *Jacques Cousteau: The Sea King; Descent: The Heroic Discovery of the Abyss,* which was a finalist for the *Los Angeles Times* Book Prize in 2006; the *New York Times* bestseller *Titanic's Last Secrets; Planet Ocean: A Story of Life,* the Sea, and *Dancing to the Fossil Record* with artist Ray Troll; the award-winning *Incredible Ocean Adventure* series for children; and many other books. He was creative producer for the *Shape of Life,* an eight-hour National Geographic television series on evolutionary biology, and has written on marine science and the environment for *Mother Jones, Audubon, Natural History,* and many other magazines. He lives on Vashon Island in Puget Sound. *Photograph by Rebecca Douglas*

ROSITA WORL, whose Tlingit names are *Yeidiklats'okw* and *Kaa.haní,* is Tlingit, *Ch'áak'* (Eagle) moiety of the *Shangukeidí* (Thunderbird) Clan from the *Kawdliyaayi Hít* (House Lowered from the Sun) in Klukwan. *Yeidiklats'okw* serves as the President of Sealaska Heritage Institute, a nonprofit that seeks to perpetuate and enhance the Tlingit, Haida, and Tsimshian cultures. She is an anthropologist and for many years served as Assistant Professor of Anthropology at the University of Alaska Southeast. *Yeidiklats'okw* has a PhD and a MS in Anthropology from Harvard University, and a BA from Alaska Methodist University. Dr. Worl has received many honors and works with several different Native organizations. She is an accomplished lecturer and author. *Photograph by David Sheakley*

JOHN SCHOEN is Audubon Alaska's Senior Scientist and co-authored a conservation assessment of the Tongass National Forest. Prior to joining Audubon in 1997, John worked for the Alaska Department of Fish and Game for 20 years as a research wildlife biologist and senior conservation biologist. He grew up on an island off the Washington coast and received his PhD in Wildlife Ecology from the University of Washington. John also serves as an Affiliate Professor of Wildlife Biology at the University of Alaska Fairbanks and has published more than 60 scientific and popular articles on Alaska wildlife. He is a Fellow of the Wildlife Society and recently received the Wilburforce Foundation's Conservation Leadership Award. John is an enthusiastic wildlife photographer and enjoys exploring Alaska's wilderness by small plane and boat. *Photograph by Mary Beth Schoen*

DOUGLAS H. CHADWICK is a wildlife biologist, natural history journalist, and founding board member of Vital Ground, a non-profit land trust that safeguards key wildlife habitat and movement corridors. He has written several hundred magazine articles on wildlife and conservation, more than fifty of them for *National Geographic* on subjects ranging from tropical beetles to snow leopards. A resident of the Glacier National Park area in

Montana, Chadwick worked many seasons in Alaska, exploring the Arctic by foot and kayak and accompanying biologists studying forests, bears, and orcas in the Tongass region. An account of the orcas there is included in his book, *The Grandest of Lives.* The latest of his eleven books, based on years of volunteer work with a research project in the Rockies, is *The Wolverine Way,* published in spring of 2010 by Patagonia. *Photograph by Rick Yates*

JOHN STRALEY is a novelist, poet, and criminal defense investigator. His first book, *The Woman Who Married A Bear,* won the Private Eye Writers of America's Shamus award for Best First P.I. Novel of 1992. His third book, *The Music Of What Happens*, won the Spotted Owl Award for Best Northwest Mystery in 1997. *Cold Water Burning,* Straley's sixth book, was nominated for Best Hard Cover P.I. Novel of 2001 by the Private Eye Writers of America. Straley's poems have appeared in various journals including: *Runes, The Alaska Quarterly Review, The Sonora Review,* and *The Seattle Times.* His essay, "Wobblies in Alaska: Who Owns an Uncaught Fish?" was published in *These United States: Leading American Writers On Their Place In the Union,* edited by John Leonard. In 2006 Straley was appointed Alaska's 12th Writer Laureate and he received an honorary doctorate from the University of Alaska, Fairbanks, in 2008. His most recent publications include the novel *The Big Both Ways* and his first collection of poems, *The Rising and The Rain.* He lives near Old Sitka Rocks in Sitka, Alaska with his wife Jan Straley and their son Finn. *Photograph by Jan Straley*

RICHARD NELSON is a writer, cultural anthropologist, and radio producer who lives in Southeast Alaska. His books include *Make Prayers to the Raven* (which became an award-winning PBS television series), *Shadow of the Hunter,* and *Patriotism and the American Land* (co-authored with Barry Lopez and Terry Tempest Williams). He received the John Burroughs Medal for *The Island Within,* the Sigurd Olson Nature Writing Award for *Heart and Blood: Living with Deer in America,* and the Lannan Literary Award for creative nonfiction; and he was the 1991–2001 Writer Laureate of Alaska. Nelson is co-producer and narrator for *Encounters,*

a nationally broadcast public radio program about the natural world. He has been a conservation activist in the Tongass National Forest for almost thirty years. For more on Richard Nelson's work as host of ENCOUNTERS, visit www.encountersnorth.org.

index

Support for *Salmon in the Trees* was made
possible through the generosity of

Campion Foundation

Wilburforce Foundation

Hugh and Jane Ferguson Foundation
North American Nature Photography
    Association Foundation
Oak Foundation
Skaggs Foundation
The Mountaineers Foundation
Weeden Foundation

BRAIDED RIVER

CHANGING PERSPECTIVES

BRAIDED RIVER,™ the conservation imprint of The Mountaineers Books, combines photography and writing to bring a fresh perspective to key environmental issues facing western North America's wildest places. Our books reach beyond the printed page as we take these distinctive voices and vision to a wider audience through lectures, exhibits, and multimedia events. Our goal is to build public support for wilderness preservation campaigns, and inspire public action. This work is made possible through book sales and contributions made to Braided River, a 501(c)(3) nonprofit organization. Please visit BraidedRiver.org for more information on events, exhibits, speakers, and how to contribute to this work.

Braided River books may be purchased for corporate, educational, or other promotional sales. For special discounts and information, contact our sales department at (800) 553-4453 or mbooks@mountaineersbooks.org.

THE MOUNTAINEERS, founded in 1906, is a nonprofit outdoor activity and conservation organization, whose mission is "to explore, study, preserve, and enjoy the natural beauty of the outdoors . . ." The Mountaineers Books supports this mission by publishing travel and natural history guides, instructional texts, and works on conservation and history.

Send or call for our catalog of more than 500 outdoor titles:

The Mountaineers Books
1001 SW Klickitat Way, Suite 201
Seattle, WA 98134
(800) 553-4453
mbooks@mountaineersbooks.org
www.mountaineersbooks.org

Manufactured in China on paper with 100% recycled content, using soy-based ink. Carbon credits were purchased to offset the emissions generated by the paper manufacturing, printing, and ocean freight.

Project Manager: Mary Metz
Acquisitions Editor: Helen Cherullo
Developmental Editor: Deb Easter
Copy Editor: Julie Van Pelt
Cover and Book Design: Jane Jeszeck/Jigsaw, www.jigsawseattle.com
Cartographer: Ani Rucki

All photographs © Amy Gulick unless otherwise noted.
Illustrations © Ray Troll.
All essays © by the author.

Front cover: Spawning chum salmon (*Oncorhynchus keta*)
Back cover: Sitka spruce tree in Auke Bay
Page 1: Black bear cub near Anan Creek
Title page: Old-growth forest on Kosciusko Island
Contents page: Bostwick Inlet estuary on Gravina Island.
Page 173: Water droplets on spent flower of villous cinquefoil
Page 175: Juvenile common mergansers (*Mergus merganser*)
Page 176: Brown bear on Admiralty Island

Library of Congress Cataloging-in-Publication Data
Salmon in the trees : life in Alaska's Tongass rain forest / Amy Gulick.
    p. cm.
  Includes index.
  ISBN 978-1-59485-091-2
 1. Natural history—Alaska—Tongass National Forest. 2. Forest ecology—Alaska—Tongass National Forest. 3. Animal ecology—Alaska—Tongass National Forest. 4. Tongass National Forest (Alaska)—Environmental conditions. I. Gulick, Amy. II. Title.

QH105.A4.S26 2010
508.798'2–dc22   2009040250

For Chris